I FEEL GREAT ABOUT MY HANDS

Edited by
Shari Graydon

I Feel Great
about My Hands

And Other UNEXPECTED *Joys of Aging*

Douglas & McIntyre
D&M PUBLISHERS INC.
Vancouver/Toronto/Berkeley

Douglas & McIntyre
An imprint of D&M Publishers Inc.
2323 Quebec Street, Suite 201
Vancouver BC Canada V5T 4S7
www.douglas-mcintyre.com

Cataloguing data available from Library and Archives Canada
ISBN 978-1-55365-786-6 (pbk.)
ISBN 978-1-55365-844-3 (ebook)

Excerpts from "Little Gidding" Part I and III in *Four Quartets*, copyright
1942 by T.S. Eliot and renewed 1970 by Esme Valerie Eliot,
reprinted by permission of Houghton Mifflin Harcourt Publishing Company.

Illustrations on pages 72–74 by Meri Collier.

Photograph on page 88 of Johanne, wrapped in the loving arms of her mom,
by Hélène Anne Fortin.

Poems by Susan McMaster (pages 212–217) and photo of Betty I.E. Page (page 210) from
Crossing Arcs: Alzheimer's, My Mother, and Me (Black Moss, 2010). Photo by Marty Gervais.
Reprinted with permission. Quotes from Betty Page.

Editing by Iva Cheung
Cover and text design by Jessica Sullivan
Cover photograph by Hélène Anne Fortin
Printed and bound in Canada by Friesens
Text printed on acid-free, 100% post-consumer paper
Distributed in the U.S. by Publishers Group West

We gratefully acknowledge the financial support of the Canada Council
for the Arts, the British Columbia Arts Council, the Province of British
Columbia through the Book Publishing Tax Credit and the Government
of Canada through the Canada Book Fund for our publishing activities.

MIX
Paper
FSC   FSC® C016245

In memory of SALLY CHRISTINE SOROKA,
*who would have enthusiastically embraced
all of the worst indignities of aging just to spend
a few more years with the people she loved.*

Contents

Introduction

My mother once remarked that she had a blast in her forties, so as I approached the milestone a little over ten years ago, I invited half a dozen slightly older friends over for dinner, insisting that, in lieu of offering anti-wrinkle cream, extra reading glasses or snarky condolence cards, they show up prepared to share with me some of the more salutary things about growing older.

You'd have thought I'd insisted they all devote their next day off to reliving the rigours of drug-free childbirth. As a face-half-unwrinkled kind of a woman, I was stunned. Even fuelled by copious quantities of wine and homemade chocolate cake, they were depressingly ill-prepared for the assignment. It was all over after a few lame references to freedom from bleeding and the joys of birth control–free sex (once every six months, whether they needed it or not). We laughed a lot despite the lamentations, but I remember thinking that I should have flown my mother in for the occasion; despite her near-blindness and bad back, she'd have done better. (Author Pearl S. Buck suggested as much, arguing, "one has to be very old before one learns how to be amused rather than shocked.")

A decade later, in July 2009, a newspaper columnist I normally read with interest devoted her twenty-four column-inches to cataloguing the litany of wrinkle-prone, gravity-challenged parts of a woman's body and the derogatory nicknames applied to each. Worse, her callous editor chose to accompany the assault with deeply unfortunate illustrations—the kind of crude line drawings you might see graffitied on the side of an abandoned meat-packing plant.

I considered writing a letter to the editor but was unable to contain the vigour of my response within the paper's dictated 250-word limit. And so I conceived of this book instead, inviting dozens of women my age or older to pen a few *bons mots* that celebrated the benefits of maturity. Envisioning a positive, multi-voiced complement to Nora Ephron's *I Feel Bad about My Neck,* I welcomed well-supported essays and creatively crafted riffs, in poetry or prose, focusing on any aspects of their journey of aging that interested my invitees. Whatever they experienced as being, gasp, even better than it used to be was fair game, and healthy doses of humour were encouraged.

The responses were as fascinatingly diverse as the women themselves. Not surprisingly, given the response to my fortieth birthday dinner, a handful declared themselves incapable of seeing the bright side of the downward slide. Family illness or the recent death of a friend often played a role. One highly placed public servant who has spent much of her career trying to rectify wrongs against the disadvantaged called me to confess that, as much as she'd like to contribute, she'd made it a practice to avoid ever publicly celebrating her good fortune. And at the other end of the empathy spectrum, a former politician—colourful, outspoken and apparently riled by the proposal—flipped me a condescending email suggesting I get a life.

But most women had an immediate and visceral positive response, easily identifying one or more issues whose benefits they had clearly already considered and were eager to share. Even those who had to work harder to see past the daily reminders of dodgy memories, fallen arches and newly insistent chin hairs expressed great appreciation at being invited to do so. The thanks I got for simply asking them to reflect and write about the uncelebrated joys of aging were heartfelt, and the insights often surprising. And for some, the act of writing itself was affirming.

More compellingly, almost every woman I spoke to during the year that it took to recruit contributors, pitch to a publisher and pull the collection together was eager to read the book when it came out—if not buy it for her mother, sister, colleague or friend.

All the authors, ranging in age from fifty to over eighty, waived royalties from sales of the book so that proceeds could benefit Media Action—the current incarnation of Media-Watch, the long-standing Canadian feminist organization that has worked for three decades to challenge the underrepresentation, stereotypic portrayal and sexual objectification of women in the media.

As MediaWatch's former president, I had passed much of the 1990s delivering media literacy presentations on related topics. These I regularly began by flashing up a picture of the latest waif supermodel and observing that, in the world of commercial media, "Women rarely live past the age of thirty-five—no doubt to avoid the utter humiliation and degradation of grey hair, wrinkles and cellulite." But the joke was all abstract theory to me at the time.

And then a year or so ago, panting in downward-dog pose after a series of strenuous sun salutations, I discovered that my knees, when pitched at a sixty-degree angle and viewed from two feet away while upside down, were surrounded by crepe-like skin that looked remarkably similar to the excessively tanned leathery stuff covering the overexposed arms of an octogenarian fruit farmer.

I was distracted by this revelation for the rest of the day and considered swearing off shorts in yoga class altogether. But then I remembered that wearing long pants would just give me more hot flashes. And—as much as I appreciate the detoxifying benefits of a good sweat, conveniently delivered with no more exertion than placing myself in close proximity to my smouldering husband or sipping a glass of red wine—I decided it was easier to just close my eyes during downward-dog pose instead.

Some of the intrepid staff at my publisher's initially questioned why I insisted that all of the book's contributors be over the age of fifty. This forced me to articulate my emerging theory on the decade of magical thinking. In my experience, ever since thirty became the new fifteen, many women in their forties don't understand that the ubiquitous terrors-of-aging messages apply to them. (Unless, of course, they've just given birth, in which case—depending on their new child's sleeping patterns and teething schedule—they may already feel more like sixty-five.)

Which isn't to say that women who haven't yet reached that mythical *certain age* are any more satisfied with their looks. Going through an old box of VHS tapes in preparation for a move recently, I stopped to view a series of commentaries I wrote and performed on CBC TV in the mid-1990s. I remembered the experience as deeply fraught. Unlike crafting arguments for the newspaper or radio, where my unshaped eyebrows or unsuitable clothing in no way interfered with the persuasiveness of my prose, TV commentary demanded an unprecedented degree of aesthetic vigilance. Borderline brilliant wit could be easily and irrevocably hijacked by wind-whipped hair, my nose in profile, or visible evidence of my face's recent intimacy with a pillow.

But as I watched the commentaries fifteen years later, what struck me more than anything was how surprisingly okay I looked—if only relative to today. What exactly was my problem? I wondered. And that's when I made the leap into the realm of French novelist Colette. It was she who famously observed, "What a wonderful life I've had! I only wish I had realized it sooner."

At that moment I vowed to keep on realizing that how I look and feel this year is likely better than I will next. As a still-healthy fifty-two-year-old, I consider my carpal tunnel syndrome, growing bunions and sensitive digestive system minor annoyances, put in context by my mother's macular degeneration, my sister's cancer and the chronic and debilitating pain felt by several friends. The time to celebrate is, indeed, now.

And whenever I find myself paying too much attention to how the previously "fine" lines around my eyes appear to have skipped right past "medium" and are moving on to "broad," I think about Kendall, the guy who served me two years ago at the RONA outlet in Kingston.

There I was, post-menopausal, makeup free and sporting my distinctive stay-warm-in-winter Walmart style, and there he was, on the phone to another outlet, trying to find out the name of a product he was recommending to me but didn't have in stock.

"Ralph, I've got a young lady here…" (Really, that's what he said: "young.")

"Oh, I don't know…" he continued, looking up at me. "I'd say about thirty-two…Yeah…Well, she's wanting some of that wood stain, you know…"

Marvelling at the sensibility of Ralph, the guy on the other end of the line who would interrupt a query about the availability of chemical in a can to ask the age of an unseen customer, I searched Kendall's friendly, lived-in face for irony or guile. Finding none, I was ridiculously gratified to conclude that he really *did* think I was thirty-two, no flattery intended. I realize he was probably suffering from untreated cataracts and likely spends all day, every day, serving grizzled male contractors, so he may not be the best judge, but I take comfort from wherever it's available.

A few of the pieces included here in the sections labelled "Desiring" and "Appearing" reminded me of Kendall. In a culture where the standard of attractiveness against which women are encouraged to measure ourselves is often defined by girls too young or too skinny to procreate, our occasional preoccupation with the state of our faces and bodies is understandable. But Britain's late Queen Mother had perspective on this. She was in her eighties when photographer Cecil Beaton offered to retouch her wrinkles. She reportedly declined, declaring, "I would not want it to be thought that I had lived for all these years without having anything to show for it."

The women whose voices are represented in this collection all have something to show for their years. And they're attentive enough to recognize the myriad advantages that accompany the accumulation of lines and the discovery through trial and humiliating error of the hairstyle that flatters them most.

As many of the contributors make clear, the perceptions of mid- to late-life women are enriched by experience; we see differently and know better, and we sometimes even benefit from the comparisons we're now in a position to make. Learning continues, advocacy efforts are enhanced, and we often appreciate more: we have the capacity to honour and celebrate others and, occasionally even, ourselves. Meanwhile, the essays in the "Surviving" section remind us that the only alternative to growing old isn't remaining young but dying before one's time.

All of the themes reflected in the organization of the book intersect, overlap and complement one another; many of the pieces could have just as easily resided under a different category. And if they occasionally express as much ambivalence as humour, they still reflect a much richer, nuanced and, yes, affirming picture of aging womanhood than I've found anywhere else.

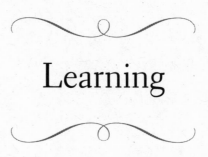

Learning

How Drooping Breasts Led Me to a Truck-driving Life of Adventure

MARLAINA GAYLE

C oming up to my forty-ninth birthday, I was dragging my ass, my teeth hurt and white wine failed to dull a chronic hip ache. Most days I surfed the web reading anything, everything to avoid doing something. I was exhausted every day and my "girls" were drooping. I felt as though I had lost my fight.

My life was pretty good. I lived in New York, had made a success out of my husband Greg's creative services business and surprised myself with my acumen in a city that's pretty tough to crack. And even though pulling up stakes at this point would mean risking the business and income I had spent ten very hard years to secure, I had a nagging feeling that I wanted to be doing something different.

Greg and I are a team in every sense of the word. Since I joined his business, we've spent 95 per cent of our time within ten feet of each other. We're a creative company of two with clients around the world. He's the president and chief creative officer and always fixes the computers; I'm the chief financial officer and director of marketing, sales and client services and also handle catering, facilities, cooking and housecleaning. The arrangement has worked well, but a few years ago, I was ready for a change.

In October 2006, my girls led the way. Midway through the month, I was slouched at my computer half-reading and vaguely listening to the TV behind me. Oprah's audience was hooting and hollering over a bunch of bras.

Most American women don't look right because they wear bras that don't fit right, Oprah announced. To prove it, she had a dozen audience members fitted with new ones. It was amazing. They looked better—a lot better. A few days later at Bloomingdale's, I was astounded to discover how good I, too, looked with the girls strapped up in a high-quality harness.

I bought four.

That was just enough of a pick-me-up to make me think I could do something about my hip. I found a chiropractor and committed myself to four weeks' worth of treatments. Now, I was looking *and* feeling better.

And that was enough to make me realize I didn't just want change—I needed adventure.

For a couple of years, Greg and I had been discussing ways to change our business. He was spending more time in front of his computer producing creative pieces and less time travelling, seeing and gathering the raw fuels for inspiration. His ass was dragging, too.

So, we wondered, could we do the same thing a different way? Should we, *could* we do something different? And if so, what?

The only thing we knew for sure was that we didn't have enough money to retire. We still needed income, so we still needed to work. And we had to do something as a team. As Greg is fond of saying, "Together, we make *one* really smart person."

We did a lot of research and wrote three business plans, but there was always a catch. We didn't want to invest our entire life savings in technology, retraining or capitalization.

We didn't want to be tied down, but we weren't ready to sever our ties to New York. We wanted to be free to travel but not have a boss, employees or customers. And we wanted to be flexible enough to continue feeding our existing business.

In January 2007, we decided our sagging asses needed immediate action, so we joined a gym. I walked the treadmill and used the weight machines five days a week. My muscles firmed up enough to warrant a new pair of Levi's. My sister-in-law told me I looked like a teenager. The new bras helped.

Six months later, Greg came home with a pile of magazines. A *Newsweek* article jumped out at me. A husband and wife team had left the corporate world to become truck drivers for Schneider National.

The idea hit me like a hammer. It was perfect! I hadn't even realized this was a job you could just apply for. Better yet, these husband and wife teams were in demand because they're used to living with each other. Two guys cooped up together in tight quarters for weeks at a time? Greg's reaction pretty much summed it up: "I'm not doing this with a dude!"

So we checked it out, even though I knew he was just humouring me.

I'm basically a pampered creature, with monthly manicures and pedicures and a penchant for Chanel-style jackets and shoes—lots of them. I also like fancy hotels and room service. I am a fair-weather everything. I sail downwind, I walk only when I won't sweat, and I only do the *après* ski thing. Besides, I hadn't driven a car in ten years. Greg did all the long-distance driving, and I was the one who cringed on the passenger side whenever he passed one of those big rigs.

But I have been known to surprise people.

Online, we found a website of current and former Schneider drivers. We found message boards, online magazines and trucker trade association sites.

We rented a car and drove out to meet a recruiter. He looked at my perky hairdo and red lipstick as I peppered him with questions. "You have a lot of energy," he said. "In three months, you'll be on that CB radio giving it to the other drivers."

By October 2007, we'd done our research and liked what we'd found:

> Team drivers earn more per mile than solo drivers. Two drivers can keep the truck moving twenty-two hours a day (gulp— that's eleven hours apiece!), twice as long as solo drivers.
> If you're on the road twenty-one days, you get four days off. twenty-eight days gets you get five.
> Pay is deposited weekly.
> Your truck gives you the equivalent of one big office window with constantly changing scenery, but no actual office. And when you get tired, your bed is right behind you.
> There's no boss to hassle with every day. Assignments come via a satellite computer and nobody talks to you unless there's a problem.
> Customers do not require follow-up. Once the freight is delivered, no one will call you. No one will ask, "Remember that trailer you delivered in California? I think it was in May. What was the weight?"

But the best news was that Schneider provided the training with no money up front.

We hummed and hawed. We were intrigued and excited, but still...

Finally, Greg put it all into perspective. "We're not quitting a job or closing our business, and we're not giving up our apartment, a certification or a licence," he said. "We are going for two weeks to try something out and see what happens. If we don't like it, we return. No one needs to know. We lose nothing and we'll have an adventure."

That sealed the deal. In January 2008, we applied to become truck drivers.

In March, after the busiest first quarter *ever* for our business, we showed up in Carlisle, Pennsylvania, for two weeks' basic training.

Four days after we arrived, we were on the road, driving a tractor-trailer under the watchful eyes of our instructors. No one knew what to make of us.

"Are you rich?" one of our classmates asked us during dinner one night. "Are you doing this for fun?"

It was a frightening, exciting and satisfying experience. I was so stressed out after my first little run behind the wheel of a big rig that I simply burst into tears. "I didn't kill anyone," I whimpered to my two instructors.

Yeah. They *really* didn't know what to make of me.

Truck drivers are not dummies. This training was the toughest thing we've ever done. We never thought it would be easy, but we had no idea just how much concentration, energy and thinking has to go into pulling the equivalent of a seven-storey building through tiny streets in little towns that were built before anyone knew what a motor car was. The responsibility is immense. It's like riding a forty-tonne rocket— and it's not easy to stop.

Navigating America's roads is further complicated by street signs that are hard to read or non-existent. There are distracted automobile drivers to contend with, along with mountains of regulations to learn. Police tend to see truck drivers as rolling piggy banks. Chances are a trucker will pay a traffic ticket because it will cost too much down time and money to fight.

"If the wheels ain't turnin', I ain't earnin'," is the mantra.

The drop-out/kick-out rate at boot camp was high. On the first day, we lost two to the physical exam. In the end, six out of the fourteen of us passed the Schneider qualifying test, and only five obtained the state Commercial Driver's License.

Double-clutching was hard enough, but turning corners was brutal. On the back of most trailers is a sign that says, "This vehicle makes wide turns." In other words, stay back! The trailer does not follow the tractor. To turn right, the driver must pull the trailer to the left so that she can get enough space to clear the corner without the trailer tires going up on the curb.

Up and down the streets of Carlisle, we were told, "Take your space, take your space." We didn't understand how this worked. No one in our families had ever pulled a camping, boat or horse trailer of any kind. The concept was completely foreign.

Despite the tears and the terror, however, we were learning together. I'd always thought we had a good marriage: we enjoyed each other's company, and we had a lot to talk about, despite living in each other's pockets for eighteen years. But spending twenty-four hours a day in a space the size of a foyer bathroom together? We shouted and screamed; we had misunderstandings. And yet the experience strengthened our marriage. I know without a doubt that he loves me absolutely.

Sharing the experience was so thrilling that if they'd kicked us out after a few days, it would still have been worth every minute.

The basic training teaches you how to drive on the street, back into a parking space and know enough about the truck's systems to know when to get it serviced. And the Schneider guys said that when they were finished with us, we would know how to be safe.

They were right.

After basic training, we became paid trainees and were given three attempts to pass the state driving test. The training cost $4,500 each, a portion of which Schneider would deduct from our paycheques for eighteen months—assuming we got licensed. If not, we'd have to pay all the money back.

Because we were a valuable husband and wife team, all of the instructors at Carlisle gave us their best. When I had trouble backing up, the sports analogies stopped and they equated the technique to piano and ballet—things I understood.

New York State has an automatic disqualification if you touch a curb, both during the driving portion and when you parallel park the sixty-five-foot truck. The first time we took the driving test, I grazed a guardrail and Greg hit a curb. The second time, we both hit the damned curb. The third time, after two weeks of driving around the quaint villages of Pennsylvania, turning, turning, turning, we passed!

On May 21, 2008, they tossed us the keys to a $120,000, 2007 Freightliner Century Class tractor and gave us a load. We were to pull forty thousand pounds of scrap paper 468 miles over the Blue Ridge Mountains of West Virginia to Owensboro, Kentucky.

The road to success is simple, our instructors told us: "Pick up on time, deliver on time, and don't hit shit." In pursuit of our new status as "professional tourists," it's a lesson we've learned well.

We have folding bikes in the tractor. We eat *hors d'oeuvres* at five o'clock when we switch drivers. The snacks include broccoli and hummus, sushi, grilled prawns and scallops on a stick, baby Roma tomatoes, goat brie and fig jam. I have discount cards at a dozen grocery chains across the United States. We pull the tractor into a grocery store parking lot every four days and stock up. It's like a perpetual camping trip. We take every bit of our time off to explore the cities and towns we stop in.

We've been to every state except Vermont and Maine and survived an ice storm in Plymouth, Indiana. I can give you directions from Boston to L.A. as though I'm telling you how to cross the street. We have hit and killed three deer—one in Wisconsin, one in Illinois and one in Montana. I hit a hawk in Pennsylvania and missed a wild pig in Texas and a goose in North Dakota. Greg skirted an alligator on I-75 in Florida.

We've seen Great Salt Lake glowing in the moonlight, Snoqualmie Pass smothered with snow in Washington State and cliffs of New Mexico bathed in the reds and purples of the sunrise.

In essence, when we drive, we are sitting on the second floor of the Interstate, where we get an incredible view. It feels like a cross between riding a horse and driving a race car. I sit high, urging my steed onward past another big truck and leaning into every curve. If I'm not one with the truck, I feel as though it will tip over.

When we first started, we drove 775 miles a day between us, and I needed a daily two-hour nap to manage my share. Today, I drive 685 miles in eleven hours. It takes us sixty hours to cross the country from New York to Los Angeles.

In October 2009, we became owner-operators by investing in our own rig—a 2007 Volvo 780 with a microwave, fridge and electricity on demand. We're hauling air freight while maintaining our old creative service business. Better yet, we're seeing the country and making money.

I've learned through all this that we get the life we create. The sappy greeting cards and cheap philosophers are right: life is about change and growth. Like most people, Greg and I got into a rut.

But if you're healthy, you can do anything. The tough part is deciding. Sometimes it's easier to figure out what you *don't* want.

I didn't want to be fifty and taking medication—or dyeing my hair, injecting Botox or getting a facelift. Now fifty-two, I've discovered I'm doing just fine. I may have grey hair, but my husband thinks I'm pretty hot sashaying around the fuel pumps in my size-eight Levi's and well-fitted bra. The other truckers open doors for me.

I wanted to be healthy and in a good and interesting marriage, with money in the bank, no debt and less stuff. I wanted off the hamster wheel but not out of the cage. I wanted freedom enough to say "fuck you" if I don't want to do something and not have to worry how I'm going to buy groceries.

I'm prepared to do things that are different and take the risks that come with choosing a new path. I still worry about having enough money for retirement and owning our own home one day. But I know that if I follow my own prescription, we'll do just fine.

Turning forty-nine forced me to change. Turning fifty set me free.

....

MARLAINA GAYLE *was an award-winning multimedia journalist and politico in Canada before moving to New York City. She was Member of the Year of the New York City chapter of the National Association of Women Business Owners, owns two successful businesses and was once a charter boat chef in the Caribbean. She blogs at www.lifewithnofixedaddress.com.*

Back to School

SUSAN DELACOURT
AND SUSAN HARADA

L et's be candid. No one wants to be known as a
"mature student."
When you're in university or college the first
time around, a "mature" person is someone who chooses to
spend the weekend at the library and arrives each week at
class with the textbook artfully highlighted in multicoloured,
neon hues. Or it's that older lady—the retired schoolteacher
perhaps, smelling faintly of lavender—who sits dutifully taking notes in your English literature classroom.

And if you choose to pursue a career in journalism, as we
did, you won't find there's much embrace of maturity there,
either. It takes a certain kind of eternal youthfulness to work
twelve- to fourteen-hour days and retain wide-eyed wonder in
response to every utterance of your interviewees. As one veteran reporter of Parliament Hill observed years ago—finding
himself squatting on his knees in front of the prime minister,
holding a radio microphone aloft—it's not a job for grown-ups.

So it wasn't a sudden fondness for maturity that sent either
of us back to university as we approached midlife. Quite the
opposite. We had maturity thrust upon us. One of us opted
to go back to school simultaneously as a professor and a part-

time master's student. The other caught the education bug while on a journalism fellowship and, inspired by her friend's example, recklessly took the plunge into a part-time master's course upon return to full-time work.

The experience, we can report, has been a little more rewarding than our foray into yoga, wherein we realized that our favourite exercises—stretching and breathing—could also be done just as well on a restaurant terrace. Why not proceed directly to the patio?

But university, the second time around, has turned us into what the social planners now call "lifelong learners." Here, for the benefit of others who may also be considering donning the mantle of maturity and going back to school, are some of the things we've learned along the way:

1. *You will go to all your classes.*
You know that dream we all have? The one where you arrive at class unprepared for an exam or realize that an assignment you haven't started yet is due? Let's just say, for one of us at least, that this is more of a real-life flashback than recurring nightmare. But when you're a "mature" student, even though you have many more legitimate reasons to miss school (work deadlines, family pressures, misplaced eyeglasses…) you won't.

Why not? On one hand, you have so much less at stake than you did the first time you went to university: your professional future won't be affected by your grades, your personal life won't depend on making new friends, the health of your finances likely won't be contingent upon maintaining a scholarship. So what's the harm of a missed class or two?

On the other hand, you are mature enough to realize—and embrace—the fact that the health of your psyche now depends on how much you continue to squeeze out of life. At your age, skipping classes is no longer value-added behaviour. Even if it means extra sleep.

Besides, you find you actually enjoy being in the class-room. It refreshes. It allows you to climb over the professional walls you've been toiling behind and root your perspective in a different spot in the world. Even if only for a few hours each week.

2. *You will hand in your assignments on time.*

It's early December, and the long-range weather forecast is calling for a blizzard mid-week—exactly the day all your final essays are due. How would we have handled this as younger students? Well, first of all, we wouldn't have known about the long-range forecast. And when the snow hit, this would be cause for celebration—a God-sent excuse to hand in the papers late.

But a "mature" student finds herself in the university park-ing lot a day before the big storm, scrambling together the change for the meter, and rushing around to shove the papers in the drop-boxes, during a stolen hour away from work.

"Is this what it means to be old?" she asks the other, upon returning from the successful drop-off.

"Yes," comes the reply. "Soon we'll be the kind of people who find ourselves sitting in the car at 5 AM, waiting to pull out of the driveway well in time for our 9 AM appointment."

This is the kind of behaviour historically associated with one's (much older, of course) parents, which you and your sib-lings long regarded as a sign of their dotage. You vowed never to be like that.

Now you view it as being unavoidably sensible—albeit a little boy-scoutish—behaviour. It is Being Prepared (for the blizzard, for the traffic jam, for the double hip replacement).

It is also acknowledgement that you have become mature enough to fully embrace the Life Is Too Short philosophy of existence. As in, life is too short to spend all that time and energy finishing your paper to deadline, only to be hit with a grade-point reduction if a whiteout prevents you from handing it in on time. You are too mature to even think of asking for an extension, should nature prevail.

You actually feel wise handling your assignment in this fashion. You try not to be openly bitter when the professor announces that, because of the snowstorm, late papers won't be penalized.

3. *You will do too much homework.*
It's Friday night and/or Saturday morning. The rest of your little family is doing normal stuff, like watching TV or working out at the gym. But you will be doing your assigned reading, over and over again, and taking copious notes. You may even feel that you need to type out the notes you took in class the week before.

If you're doing an essay, your bibliography will stretch over pages and pages, and you will have actually read the sources you cite. Yes, you've now become that kid who spent all her time at the library—the one with the multicoloured notes.

At the next class meeting, the professor will start to ask questions based on the readings. You will sit, tensely, as the questions are greeted with abject silence by the other students. Being older, and remembering what it was like to be younger, you don't want to be that annoying person who puts up her hand and says "oh, I know" every time the teacher speaks. But as the seconds tick by, you weigh that scenario against the roar of silence. Are you the only one who feels awkward? Yes you are. And then you'll answer the professor's question. And she or he will invariably respond (somewhat ungratefully, it should be noted) that your answer is only partly correct, or way off. So the next weekend, you'll take even more notes while your family is off enjoying itself in leisure pursuits. And so it goes.

4. *You are your own adult supervision.*
Remember when your dad or mom saw your marks and would ask, "What happened to that other 10 (20, 25) per cent?" Now, you simply eliminate the middle person and ask yourself, directly, the same question. Comfortingly, perhaps, you have no better answer today than you did when your parents asked.

Then again, the answers you do eventually arrive at in the middle of the night will be brutally honest. Being mature can give you clearer insight into the options you face and the choices you wind up making, given the variables you have to juggle.

You calculate to the second how much time must be devoted to each assignment in order to lay crucial research groundwork for your future thesis and earn the highest grades possible, while still allowing yourself to enjoy the learning process, spend time with your family and fulfill the duties of your full-time job. You learn to be kind to yourself about the missing 10 (or 20 or 25) per cent.

5. *You will adjust your fashion sense.*
What are the young people wearing these days? Pretty much what you were wearing when you went to school. Jeans, sweaters, and such. Nothing to see here. It's school, not a fashion show. Get back to studying. And try not to dwell on the fact that you are wearing the same sweater as the nineteen-year-old sitting beside you. Remind yourself that you are mature, and with maturity comes the ability to laugh at yourself. Just remember to do it before everyone else does.

6. *You will realize that young people really are young.*
While on campus, any sentence beginning with "back when I first went to university" can be a real conversation stopper, and thus you refrain from saying it aloud most days. But it strikes you that students look much younger than they did

back when, well—when you first went to university. You are not imagining it. They are younger; in Ontario, for example, many of them show up on campus at the tender age of seventeen. Your couch is older than that, for heaven's sake. But you are mature enough to realize that this, too, is a conversation stopper.

7. *You will rediscover a taste for beer.*
At some point, if you do decide to join your younger classmates for a beverage after class, there's good news and bad news. Bad news—there's no wine list. In fact, there's no wine. Just beer. And for God's sake don't ask for wine. You will be mocked. Good news—they're still playing the same music they played at the student pub when you were at school. It seems that, unlike you, Bachman-Turner Overdrive and the Steve Miller Band never got old.

8. *You will experience jet lag, without the benefit of travel.*
Someone quite wise (i.e., older than us) once remarked that young people live in a different time zone. Very true. You will quickly come to realize that if you are Eastern Standard, for example, you can assume their lives are set to a Pacific Standard clock.

Therefore, you will refrain from suggesting that you and the younger members of your study group meet at the library at 8 AM. If you are out for an after-class beverage with them (see point 7, above), you will restrain yourself from ordering hefty food items even though it's 6:30 PM and you're really hungry. You will muffle your gasp of horror when they talk about meeting up later for dinner at, say, 9:30 PM. You will not allow your laughter to cross the fine line from genuine amusement to hysteria when it strikes you that although they regularly climb into their beds at about the same hour you're rolling out of yours, they still look much younger.

9. *You will dwell in a foreign land—*
   again, without the benefit of travel.

It is unsettling to discover that, upon venturing onto campus from the world of journalism (or from the world of anywhere else, for that matter), you do not understand much of what's being said by the students around you. You also find yourself parsing the same sentence over and over, as you try to decode the dense words of your assigned readings.

Do not despair. It is not a sign of maturing (read aging) cognitive abilities. You see, in addition to standard English and French, a number of other languages are usually employed at universities. There is the young people language. And there is the academic one, complete with numerous dialects tied to subject areas, equally unintelligible to the outsider.

Being mature, you have the perseverance to grasp the latter language—the one used within your own academic subject area specialty—and on good days, in the heat of the moment, you might even sound and/or write like a local.

The former, not so much. Don't even try.

10. *You will make friends with footnotes.*

In journalism, it is very cool to keep your sources secret. In university, that is definitely not on. The sweeping attribution "according to sources" is not an acceptable term in academia.

Although you may have made your living in communications, you are going to have to learn to write all over again. Lesson number one is that it takes about as long to cite sources properly as it does to write the essay. Be mature enough to not apply the Life Is Too Short philosophy here (as in, life is too short to spend whole days formatting citations).

In the world of academia, a properly formatted citation is a beautiful thing, and you really should have the maturity to appreciate this.

11. *You will try to remember your fellow*
    students mean well when they say…
    "I was three when you got your BA."
        "Did you actually cover Brian Mulroney?"
        "No way." (When you tell them you used to smoke in the
    classroom.)
        "How would you do an essay on a typewriter?"
        "My brother is the same age as your son."
        "I know you're a journalist. We used your stuff in my high
    school history class."
        (And, especially crushing) "My mom says exactly the same
    thing."

    And so.
    When we set out to describe our experience, we decided
we wanted to start from a non-aging perspective. Not to offer
advice on how to handle aging but on how you may discover
the need to calibrate and recalibrate (and, in the process,
strengthen) your sense of self while travelling through other
worlds dominated by younger people.
    We both entered the journalistic workforce at an early age.
We were always among the youngest, if not the youngest, in
our respective newsrooms. Sure, we got older as years went
by, but so did our older colleagues. Even though new young
reporters began surfacing at the news conferences and scrums
on Parliament Hill, they remained the minority.
    That's why we were in for a bit of a perceptivity shock
when we arrived on campus. Someone had turned the totem
pole of age upside down, and suddenly we were at the bottom.
    Never mind. Journalism demands, if nothing else, the
honing of mental focus as an essential survival skill. We
focused on our new personas as mature students and took on
the experience as a challenge to be met with humour, insight
and perspective.

On the days (and there will be days) when those mature attributes fail you, you will learn to reach for the truisms and clichés. And then—smug in the knowledge that fine wine improves with age, and mindful that one is only as old as one feels—you will adjust the font size on your laptop, pack up your multicoloured highlighters and set off for class much too early, resolutely heading once more unto the breach.

Above all else, you will learn that going back to school is a very good idea.

SUSAN DELACOURT *is a prominent political journalist* (Globe and Mail, Ottawa Citizen, Toronto Star) *and author* (United We Fall, Shaughnessy: The Passionate Politics of Shaughnessy Cohen, Juggernaut: Paul Martin's Campaign for Chrétien's Crown). *She plans to be winding up her master's degree by the time you read this, right on deadline.*

SUSAN HARADA *was a national reporter for* CBC TV, *specializing in justice and defence issues. She also did stints in foreign reporting and as occasional anchor of* The National *and* The Journal. *She joined Carleton University's journalism faculty in 2003 and obtained her Master's in Legal Studies in 2008.*

Why I Colour My Hair

SUSAN MERTENS

Life is lived forward but understood backward.
Søren Kierkegaard

It's Saturday morning. I'm sitting under a hair dryer with a plastic bag on my head. The magazine cover on my lap shows a coronation portrait of the young Queen Elizabeth II alongside a contemporary shot of the monarch in full state regalia. I'm reading the horoscopes.

At my feet, in my purse, is a notebook. In it are jottings and false starts for what I hope will one day be my personal version of a grand unified theory. Not in physics but aesthetics. I always bring it to the salon. I travel hopefully.

I've downgraded my immediate ambition to chronologically mapping my philosophical enthusiasms, distinguishing crushes from enduring relationships. It's the intellectual equivalent of buying a closet organizer (which I've also recently done). Failure to progress on either front is attended by guilt. I'm very aware that horoscope reading is an avoidance activity.

Another brain circuit is thinking how little this salon ritual has changed. It could be my mother sitting here having postpartum grey rinsed away after my birth. Despite the rollover of the century, even the magazine contents would seem familiar to her. So would my contradictory mix of rationales for covering up "my wisdom," as one friend calls her white hair.

I wonder what my mother would be thinking about in my place. I drift. My attention skips, like a needle on vinyl, and time, suddenly, telescopes.

The years between 1952, the date of my birth, and this sunny Saturday simply cease to matter. The particulars of my life story, the narrative (or today's version) from which my sense of self-identity normally hangs, are of no consequence to me. The noisy demand for individuality has gone quiet.

This sort of thing has been happening to me a lot lately. It's quite pleasant—a fact that surprises me, because the first time something similar occurred at age twenty, it felt like a free fall into the abyss. Back then, a psychiatrist diagnosed an identity crisis.

So what happened along the way to replace the terror of personal annihilation with this cheerful embrace of egoless being?

Damned if I know.

Damned if I know why, at this stage of life, I'm cycling through larva-pupa-butterfly metamorphoses out of sequence and out of season.

Consider an experience I had two years ago, when, for month after magical month, I was the calm, positive, in-the-moment person of my imaginings. Day-to-day irritations didn't ruffle my mood. My beloved would lose his temper; I'd feel an uncharacteristic wave of tenderness. I was soothing and reasonable. I counselled friends who actually listened for once because they'd noticed the change in me too.

This wasn't an instant of insight like today in the salon. I had felt it coming on for some time—like a head cold. The absences were what I noticed first. Absence of indignation, anger, jealousy. I thought of the Bible verse about love being slow to anger. I became increasingly reluctant to judge others (unusual, you'll agree, for someone who used to earn her keep as a music critic).

Then unfamiliar symptoms began. I experienced humbleness. Not chagrin. Not a dip in self-esteem. Humbleness as in "Aren't we all just trying to cope as best we can with the understanding we have at the moment?"

A generalized caring flooded in. It washed over strangers and acquaintances, animals and plants alike. I was in a stupor of serenity. Then it gradually ebbed away. The level in the reservoir of patience dropped. And, one day, I found myself as irritable and moody as my seventeen-year-old self.

Compassion was back to colliding with accountability. It felt as though I'd been on a holiday from my humanity and had to become comfortable with being uncomfortable again. But, perhaps perversely, the familiar sense of struggle, of a conflicted selfhood, felt more right now, more natural. Even necessary.

What I took away from my year of magical thinking was that learning does feel like struggle. Yet it's what we're most suited to do. After decades envying other species their wholeness, the intrinsic aesthetic beauty of their running or their flight, I understand now that ours is a learning species.

With our complex neural circuitry and plasticity of brain function, there is beauty inside our skulls. And every day we are shown new representations of that beauty as scientists— and philosophers—explore inner space with functional MRIs and other high-tech products of our imaginations.

I understand why my aging brain requires more novelty to focus my attention, why time seems to have sped up, why I need a nap after being in a high-stimulus environment. I understand that my (fitful) ability to be in the eternal now is not the pinnacle of human achievement. Holding past, present and future in my mind simultaneously, applying experience and projecting imagined possibilities, learning, understanding—*there's* the wonder that Francis Bacon called the seed of knowledge.

So despite nagging concerns that I know this plot and have seen the movie (both the original and the remake)... despite loss of every conceivable kind... despite all the flux I've experienced in my fifties, wonder is in plentiful supply. I'm even, occasionally, blithe.

And we didn't do blithe in my family growing up. My mother was a chronic worrier; my father's mother retreated into a generalized anxiety disorder when she was my age; my father self-medicated. I'm the beneficiary of newer drugs and analysis. I'm getting better at getting out of my own way.

I can be content with not having the answers. Asking the question really *is* enough some days. Knowing that I don't know, though I might—or might not—at some future point, creates neither anxiety nor frustration (those bosom companions of my youth).

Experience has taught me not to be surprised when insight and understanding enter through the unlikeliest doors and windows. Or, as Leonard Cohen has it, through the cracks in everything.

Which is another reason I'm reading the Jonathan Cainer horoscopes in *Hello!* magazine this sunny Saturday. My husband calls horoscopes tripe. In a misspent journalistic youth, he briefly wrote them for a magazine not unlike this one, so he thinks he knows.

It may appear that I've set the big philosophical questions aside. I don't teach. I don't publish. But I contemplate—a rare vocation these days. I try to understand the significance of the seemingly insignificant detail and put it into the wider context of a life.

Like a February horoscope that reads:

Some things in life just aren't worth thinking about. Why, then, think about them at all? While it's interesting to every so often contemplate a deep question, you need to be aware that you are probably never going to reach a fully satisfactory answer. The best you can attain is a new conceptual picture that will serve you well until you eventually outgrow it. Let yourself think what you want, but, more importantly, allow yourself to acknowledge what you truly feel. Only then will you understand what you most need to understand.

Just kidding. That isn't my horoscope. It's my husband's.

My horoscope, in contrast, perfectly catches the muddle of *tristesse* and hope that leads me, among other things, to colour my hair:

If you are too eager to embrace your next opportunity, you won't apply enough discrimination. But if you think you have nothing to look forward to, think again. Think of how good things could be, how well they could turn out, how smoothly and swiftly problems could be solved. Don't jump to pessimistic conclusions. Indeed, steer clear of negative assumptions and critical judgments. Keep an open mind and you'll soon see reason to open your heart. Something, somewhere up there, wants only the best for you.

Next month, it will be different.

....

SUSAN MERTENS *is a Toronto-born former* CBC *Radio arts journalist and dance and music critic for the* Vancouver Sun *who was permanently sidelined by illness at the age of thirty-five while pursuing a PhD at the University of British Columbia. She celebrates the contemplative life with her husband, Max, and dog, Zeus, in Lions Bay, B.C.*

A *Club* of One's Own

BETH ATCHESON

When I turned fifty-five, I decided that for once in my life I should do an impetuous thing. I went even further: I did an impetuous thing that was out of character for a game-hating person, contra-indicated by my osteoarthritis and questionable to my feminist politics.

I took up golf, the favourite game of the patriarchy: older white men of privilege wearing white shoes and belts, chasing a white ball. Now I am an older white woman of privilege who occasionally wears white (for the first time in my life), chasing a ball that is not always white and softer than the ones the men play. And I like it, most of the time. Which is how much I like most else I do. Most of the time is apparently also how much anyone else likes golf.

What was I thinking?

Well, I must admit I was thinking *only* of myself. No mistake—I have led a good life, and I often think of myself, do good things for myself. But I have fitted them into a busy life where I am also doing things because:

> I've always done them, and my roles in my extended family are fixed.
> I choose to do them for my nuclear family.

> I must do them for my job or boss.
> I want to change the world as a feminist activist.
> I feel guilty—period!

Golf I am doing *only* for myself, and that makes it different; it is too hard to do for any other reason, especially if you take it up at age fifty-five. But this is a reward of aging—seeing the possibility, time and space to do something just for ourselves, often something new and unexpected. We can be different than we have been.

I found a club with a welcoming women's division and wonderful members where many are starting later in life, travelling the same golf path, at least for a while.

For me, the point of golf is the companionship. If golf were played alone, it would not be nearly so popular nor so enjoyable. Related to the companionship is eating and drinking—in moderation, of course. At my club, there is a further extension to dancing, but I know when not to push my luck.

When I am pushing away from my desk to go play golf, I am thinking about the smiles that will inevitably greet me as I walk down the hill to the first tee, from Holly, Kathy and Barb. I am thinking about how we will encourage each other as we hit our way down (often around, with a stop at the beach in the bunkers) the fairway to the green. I am thinking about how much we will laugh as we three-putt (fish tales also are frequent in golf; it might have something to do with being in the water a lot) our way to the hole. (Of course, we would like to play better—without practising, although we're starting to understand the relationship.) That is another reward of aging—that one can find pleasure in the moment, storing the best moments for ballast when everything is upturned, which it can do at any age but seems to happen more regularly when you have teenage children and aging parents at the same time.

In addition to wanting to do something only for myself, I wanted to do something that was purely fun. Now, with some experience, I have concluded that golf does not meet this particular criterion. But it comes close enough. One of my very favourite things is to learn from the women around me and to integrate that knowledge of women's experiences into my legal and public policy work. I always come away from a game with something new to think about. Kathy is teaching me about the complexity of running daycares, Holly is educating me about what makes for successful retail sales, and Barb provides unusual and creative ways to look at familiar things.

You have to take life as it comes, figure out what to do and accept the consequences. Golf is similar: the ball is supposed to be played where it lies. This fundamental rule leads to some of the funniest moments in any round of golf. But the consequences are never as significant as they can be in real life—though you might not know that from the way some golfers behave after a shot. Ben Hogan, a great American player from the twentieth century, said that he played with friends, but they did not play friendly games. If that happens to me, much of the magic of golf would be gone, and I might have to switch to biathlon.

In my mid-fifties, I was feeling a little stale, a little bored, a little unchallenged. Doing more of the same had no attraction. Introducing a new and unpredictable, but still manageable, activity has had benefits I didn't foresee. The simple act of getting outside, of breathing more fresh air, of changing what I see, gives me more energy to come back and tackle the things in life I find hard. In the process, I've been reminded to always look beyond the stereotypes—golf has more than its fair share—to absorb the history and character of the game and the people in it. I am navigating a whole new and unfamiliar social space.

And yet I have a nagging feeling of guilt about playing golf, especially because I joined a private club. By all the standard measures, I am a privileged person. Much of what I have is the result of hard work, but I have greatly benefited from good fortune and the support of others. Golf is not the closed space it once was—it's changed dramatically over the last century as class, race and gender have pushed it open. But I feel a tension that I don't expect to go away, and perhaps that's a good thing. If I am tempted to take the golf experience for granted, to treat it as my due, to complain about it, my conscience will prick the golf bubble and push me back into life on this complex shared planet.

I do agree very much with the spirit of something else Ben Hogan said. He declared that the most important shot is the next one. As I age, it is tempting to second guess myself and my past choices, to mull over expectations and relationships. I like the feel of focus, forward momentum, positive possibility and mystery as to what will happen, in my golf game and in my life.

....

BETH ATCHESON, *a native of New Brunswick, is now a lawyer who lives in Toronto with her lawyer/golfer husband and musician son. She has had a career in private practice, government and the non-profit sector. Beth is a long-time advocate for equality for women and girls.*

Karate for Felix, Tai Chi for Me

LIZ WHYNOT

Felix has been taking karate classes at Vancouver's West End Community Centre, something my partner, his birth granny, did thirty years ago. Not to be outdone, I joined up too.

I remember those classes well. The club was established by an Okinawan sensei I never met who, I was told, was a professor at a local university. He studied why people make war, they said. Both Japanese and non-Japanese black belts taught us. One of them was a strutting Vancouver police-man who later accumulated notoriety for his opinions about how to address the intractable social issues on Vancouver's Downtown Eastside. I completely disagreed with him on that front.

Not surprisingly, this was a pretty macho club. They did teach us a basic tenet of karate—that, through calmness and awareness, it is possible to deflect conflict and never use one's skills. But those skills were developed in a highly competitive environment, a lot like the military training in *An Officer and a Gentleman*, I thought.

We were worked out in unison—loudly counting *"ichi, ni, san, shi"*; applying ourselves vigorously to the sit-ups and push-ups, kicks and punches; focusing fiercely our *ki* and our *kiais.* I was about thirty at the time and ate this up like soup. I really wanted to be as trim and fit and hard as the men—or at least as the women black belts, who were every bit as macho as the guys. I was—still am—a very, very competitive person. Richard Gere had nothing on me.

And the classes were exciting. Everyone wore white *gis,* everyone worked through repetitive and ritual movements, and everyone felt the same interesting undercurrents of competition (and probably sexual tension) as we strove for approval from the teachers. Every once in a while, we had to show what we'd learned by performing a set of exercises—a kata—and if we did that right, we were given a different coloured belt. I am competitive, but I am not athletic—not really. I managed a green belt from that club and then, inevitably, I stopped going... can't remember why. The teachers changed or something. I kept the belt for ten years, unwilling to give up the vision of my hard, flexible, speedy, coordinated self. It's actually possible that I still have it somewhere and will locate it at the back of the drawer in my old desk when I get to the next stage of reducing my possessions.

So Felix said, "I want to show you my kata." Well, he can show me anything but the latest Mario Brothers and I'm interested.

"Go for it," I said. And there it all was, Heian Shodan, kata number one, performed perfectly in the spiky precise efficient way he was trained. It took me right back, of course, to doing that one myself, and soon I'll remember the three or four others I learned before I gave up on mastering side kicks and quit.

"Nice work," I said. "Do you want to see my tai chi set? That's sort of a kata."

"How many moves?" he asked.

"One hundred and eight. And we do it slower."

"Uh. No thanks."

I was a bit disappointed, though I suppose a ten-year-old black belt video gamer like Felix couldn't be expected to sit through the twenty embarrassing minutes the set would have taken.

I have been doing tai chi for about a year. I chose it because I needed to improve my balance, damaged by a benign tumour that grew on my right vestibular nerve, which, combined with the effects of treatment, has also left me deaf on that side. As I said to a friend, all I was really hoping for was to be able to stand on one foot again, without hanging on to the towel rack when getting out of the bathtub. I explained this in response to his observation that the type of tai chi I had chosen was not really as authentic as others. A lifelong devotee of the martial art, he said, "No one recognizes that form, you know."

Oh well. By the time he told me that, I had figured out that, whatever form it was, it actually worked for me. And anyway, no one there had mentioned anything about recognition—only general encouragement to show up for classes or attend weekend workshops.

That's not to say that I didn't bring the same old competitive self to the classes when I started. In spite of quite concrete physical evidence to the contrary—going deaf, sagging jowls (and other things), various herniated discs—I carried my old myth of physical ability and indestructibility along with me, wrapped up in my need to look good in my stretch pants.

Sure enough, I learned the general moves pretty easily; some of them are quite like karate moves. I progressed faster than most in the beginners' group (and looked good doing it, I thought). Regardless of looks or finesse, however, at the end of three months, all the beginners were invited into the continuing class, where the drill was to hone in on individual moves, analyze them in great detail and then repeat them a lot of times. This is where it gradually dawned on me that although I had learned the general directions of the 108 moves, I didn't actually know much at all. The great teaching of tai chi for me is that in slowing down and rehearsing and rehearsing the smallest moves, I develop a deeper understanding at the same time as I recognize how superficial that understanding remains.

As the months went by, I became more aware of the other people in the class. Most of us are over fifty, I would say, though there are some in their thirties and forties. Our various backgrounds reflect the ethnic and racial makeup of Vancouver. I'm not sure if any who attended would ever have seen themselves as athletic, though certainly there are some who seem a bit more coordinated than others. But the magic is that we are all doing the same thing, usually a hundred times, in the ways that each of us is able. A hundred knee bends. A hundred Cloud Hands. A hundred Step Back Repel Monkeys. And it apparently doesn't matter how many times we do it or have done it; we still need to do it again. Because of the possibilities that emerge for feeling it differently, for doing it more deeply. And we do it together.

There are lots of classes. I had committed myself to one a week, Tuesday afternoon. However, I got a job, sort of, and had to find another class, so I showed up on a Thursday. I lined myself up near the back and prepared to do the set when the wrinkled woman next to me said to me in her harsh, affirmative crone's voice, "Who are you?"

"Liz," I said, "from Tuesday."

"Oh. Well, welcome to Thursday." And we all started again, arm exercises, leg exercises, two sets, turns. I felt very happy to be there.

Later someone told me that the woman who spoke to me was eighty-nine years old. My father died last year, and he was eighty-nine. She knew the set and did it as well as anyone. And I realized that we could say the same about all of us. We were happy to be there, and we were learning together, and no one gave a damn about how we looked or how well we were doing it in relation to each other. No competition. Just gratitude that we could do this, and keep on doing it, and it would never be finished. No belts of any colour. Just a different ugly T-shirt each year and some soft cotton pants if you wanted.

The other thing I realized was that I am now one of them. I am older than I used to be. My body is different, and I am different. I am glad to join the elders who persist in learning the moves, in slowing it all down to feel and understand the parts.

As for Felix, I hope he has a healthy, athletic, artistic and exciting life. And one day, I hope he discovers, sooner than I did, the plain joy of doing something slowly—just for the felicity of it.

LIZ WHYNOT *retired in 2008 after eight years as the leader of B.C. Women's Hospital and Health Centre. Prior to that, she had worked as a general practitioner and a public health doctor. A co-founder of Vancouver's Sexual Assault Service and the Sheway Program, Liz received the Kaiser Foundation National Award for Leadership in 2009.*

Appearing

A Woman over
the Preschool Age

SUSAN MUSGRAVE

"Distrust any enterprise that requires new clothes," advised Henry David Thoreau. One of the high points of the writing life is that every time you sit down to start work on a new book, you don't have to go shopping, first, for a new wardrobe. As long as you work at home, you don't even need to dress respectably.

But the downside to being a writer is that every so often you are obliged to leave the house—to give readings, lead writing workshops or promote your latest *tour de force*. I was shocked, recently, by a fellow poet-doyenne with whom I'd been invited to appear on the Fashion Channel. "What are you going to wear?" she asked.

I hadn't given it a thought; I'd been too preoccupied thinking about what I was going to say. My friend said it didn't matter what I said; as long as I looked good and dressed well, I could probably get away with saying nothing. But would anyone buy my book, I wondered, if I appeared on the Fashion Channel with my dressing gown on inside out?

Gore Vidal said to never miss a chance to have sex or be on television. I decided to stick with radio. I didn't want viewers calling in to say, "She looks ugly, and her mummy dresses her funny." I remembered when Barbara Frum moved from radio to television, and everyone started criticizing her for her taste in tops. Countries were being bombed, children blown up, and she'd be live on the scene asking an overthrown dictator if he was bitter. The rest of us would be criticizing her wardrobe, saying, "Barbara's shoulder pads are lopsided; she really shouldn't wear taupe at her age; that bow at her throat makes her look choked."

I told the producer I'd never missed a chance to have sex— it's one enterprise that does not require clothes, let alone any new ones—but I didn't think I was ready to bare my soul on television, yet.

When it comes to haute couture, I'm like Gilda Radner: I base my fashion taste on what doesn't itch. What doesn't itch translates to clothes that fit comfortably and keep me warm. My office has heat, but when you have a sedentary job and poor circulation, your extremities get cold.

The first thing I do, before going to work, is fix a hot water bottle for my feet. Then—and I know this could make Gilda start itching in her grave—I slip on my coarse wool underwear. There's no chance of falling asleep over my iBook—I keep myself awake by scratching.

On top of the Stanfields, I add the hand-knit wool sweater I bought high up in the Andes—the kind that is meant to keep you warm when you run out of coca leaves to chew. I squeeze into my favourite pair of jeans and accessorize with two pairs of work socks and a pair of fuzzy pink slippers. For the final layer, my white virgin wool dressing gown—in case an Arctic draft sweeps my office and the sweaters and the Stanfields aren't enough.

They say you lose a good deal of heat through the top of your head, and in that area I can't afford to lose anything more. I wear the toque my mother knitted (with fingerless mitts to match) that has a bell attached to the pom-pom. Handy, if I've stopped itching long enough to start nodding off.

I CONFESS I don't know any writers who've died of exposure, at least not while at their desks, but I'm not taking any chances. The other day, I got up from the couch where I was resting before my coffee break and found a courier at the door. He looked me up and down. "Did I get you out of bed?" he said. I don't know too many people who get out of bed at four in the afternoon dressed to survive the Franklin expedition, but I could be out of touch with current trends.

The comfortable look has caused other, familial, problems. Years ago, when I used to pick up my daughter from daycare, she begged me to "dress fancy" when I came for her, "like the real mothers do." The other mothers, it was true, dressed as if they'd just come from the kinds of jobs real people have: lawyers, dentists, teachers, shopkeepers—people for whom growing up included learning to dress themselves.

I thought I'd made concessions: before going to fetch my daughter, I always took off the slippers and put on a pair of gumboots—two left feet I bought at a garage sale on the Queen Charlottes twenty years ago. I changed out of my dressing gown into a lime green Mustang floater jacket I bought at the same sale (I got a great package deal). But my daughter said the jacket was not cool. My mother agreed. She said if I checked the label, it would probably be past its expiry date.

I went a step further in my attempts to be, if not a real mother, a good one. Before driving to Rainbow Daycare, I slipped out of everything comfortable and put on pantyhose, a skirt, a blouse, a pair of shoes with heels, makeup, even a touch of lipstick. I didn't want to cause my daughter further embarrassment and have her sue me, in later years, for a wrecked childhood. There was only one other problem. It was a lot easier getting out of the car when I was dressed, comfortably, in my sweater and jeans.

Our car needed a few repairs. Neither of the doors opened, so you had to climb in and out through the hatchback. But my daughter didn't seem to be concerned about that. It was the clothes, she claimed, that made me stand out from everyone else.

A couple of years ago, my mother dragged me into an upscale boutique to buy a dress, a most humbling and humiliating experience. The occasion? I'd been invited to have lunch with the Queen.

I argued that I already owned a dress—one my daughter had bought with her hard-earned allowance, at the Previously Loved Shop in Sidney. It was a synthetic material, with a houndstooth-patterned camel-coloured skirt and an off-cream-coloured blouse that fastened with a little bow at the throat, and it might have suited me if I'd been a depressed bank teller in the '30s. I wept when she gave it to me. I mean, was this who she wanted me to be? Or worse, was this who she thought I was?

I have never worn the dress. I told her it was too precious for every day, that I was saving it for an important event. A funeral. My own. I know women often want to be buried in their wedding dress—a custom that draws some alarming comparisons between marriage and death—but I don't want to spend eternity as a bride. I'd sooner be buried in my bathing suit—though who knows if I even own one anymore. I dare say the light in a coffin six feet under would be more flattering than the fluorescent light above a change room when you go to try on a bathing suit.

I don't like shopping at the best of times. To begin with, I'm a difficult fit—my waist isn't where it's supposed to be, my breasts are as lopsided as Barbara Frum's shoulder pads, and I have hips—something contemporary moulders of fashion don't seem to take into account when they design dresses for women over the preschool age.

It doesn't matter what you try on; there is always a salesclerk to tell you, "That is *so* you!" as if she has seen into the depths of your essence based on an exchange of pleasantries: "Good morning, may I help you?" "No thanks, I'm just looking." And if "me" is the woman in the mini sailor dress who looks like Shirley Temple forty years after the *Good Ship Lollipop* left port, I want to be someone else anyway.

I might have bought the mini sailor suit, because—apart from the length—it fit (my definition of a dress that fits is one that I can zip up myself, without help from anyone else, while I'm still vertical), but I took it off the moment the salesclerk told me it looked "hot." "Hot" was not the effect I wanted when I dined at Government House with the Royals.

The next boutique my mother and I "nipped into" was even more ostentatious. The kind of place where the haves and the have mores, as George Bush calls his friends, would shop. The salesclerk looked as though she had stepped out of a *Sports Illustrated* swimsuit issue and had been trained to make everyone else feel that good about herself. "You'd be a size three," she enthused. How could she tell when I hadn't even unzipped my Mustang floater jacket?

"Try sixteen," I said, modestly. Even Tropical Beach Barbie would have to have liposuction to get into a three.

The salesgirl insisted a five would swim on me. I said I wanted something very basic, very black, that covered everything between my neck and my ankles, but that, she had decided on her own, was not the real me. She brought me a gown made of silk pongee with metallic silver thread woven through the bodice, "just in from Europe," for $2,100. "That's definitely you, so feminine and romantic," she said.

I felt naked. I hadn't fooled her a bit. She'd seen through my two left-footed gumboots, blue jeans, Chilean sweater and lime green floater jacket to the feminine romantic soul of a poet I was underneath.

The colour of the dress reminded me of the last time I splurged on a dozen raw oysters and regurgitated the lot. And

$2,100 seemed a bit much, considering the dress was run-up by loving hands at home (everything in the boutique was "original and handmade"). Still, knowing it meant a lot to the clerk (in terms of a commission) I agreed to try it on under one condition: she didn't tell me how hot I looked when I emerged from the change room. I told her I understood it was her job to flatter me so that I would spend obscene amounts of money but that I had a hard time being obscene under pressure.

"I promise I won't say a word," the salesclerk told me. "Just do your thing."

Before I had even got the zipper on my Mustang floater jacket unstuck, she was hovering at the cubicle door. "How does it fit? Do you need any help in there? I brought you a few other... more mature sizes... just in case." I would have needed help getting my leg through the waist of the size-three dress, so I accepted the adult sizes.

THERE ARE NO mirrors in change rooms for a good reason: you have to come out and embarrass yourself in front the staff and all the other customers, who ogle your inevitably unshaved legs with the dents in them from the tube socks you've been wearing all day (and in my case the whole night before, in bed). There is one certainty about trying on new clothes: you are never wearing the appropriate footwear. If it's something feminine and romantic, you can be sure you'll be wearing two left-footed gumboots when you nip in to try it on.

I didn't need to expose myself to the trick mirror outside the change room to know my instincts were right and that something black and size sixteen would have shown off my full figure to full advantage. I tried to imagine driving up to Government House for my date with Her Majesty, when I realized why I was feeling so dizzy: the change room curtains were made of the same material as my dress. Standing in front of the curtains, I looked like a disembodied head. I supposed it wouldn't have mattered once I'd left the boutique, but I couldn't help but wonder if they had made the curtains and then had enough material leftover for a dress, or if it was vice versa. The salesclerk went cross-eyed, looking at me as if I were an optical illusion. Finally, she said, "I know I promised—but can I say one thing?" Without waiting for me to say, "Let me guess, I blend with the decor," she said, "The colour looks very cool on you."

I agreed to take the dress, as long as my mother didn't subject me to any more shopping, but she had one further item on her list—a coat. I took her point—the Mustang floater jacket on top of the silk pongee number made me look like a person of no fixed address who pushes her oddments around town in a stolen shopping cart. "What happened to you?" my daughter said, when I got home and modelled my new faux fur for her. I surveyed myself in my full-length mirror, one I have learned to trust. I looked like a full-figured five-foot-six marmot.

When the big day came and I arrived at Government House, I was shown to my table and seated for lunch. I kept my coat firmly buttoned, and no one offered to take it from me. Perhaps they figured—my being a writer known for flouting social convention—I might not have had anything on underneath.

After knocking back a glass of wine or two, I felt relaxed (and hot) enough to think about undoing a top button. But then Her Majesty entered the ballroom wearing the same dress as I had on, the regurgitated oyster–coloured gown, made of silk pongee with metallic silver thread woven through the bodice, just in from Europe.

I erred on the side of diplomacy and kept my coat severely buttoned to the neck as I made light conversation with her in between mouthfuls of chicken cordon bleu. I asked her if she had to take Prozac to survive lunches such as this, and did she ever feel like strangling her husband? I'd seen the film *The Queen*, where he'd disparaged the late Diana, and thought it a bit much. Somebody, her personal secretary perhaps, answered for her, not even giving her a chance to get a word in edgewise. I could tell, by the way she stared straight through me, she coveted my faux coat.

I never wore the silk dress again, but two days later, I went to visit my husband in prison and wore the fur. If nothing else, I thought, it would give the guards something to talk about. "How are we supposed to know it's you, without that old floater coat." "Who died and made you Queen?" That sort of lively banter.

I was sitting in the visiting room sharing a tuna melt with my husband when he pointed at my sleeve and said, between mouthfuls, "What's that?" I looked down. My coat still bore its price tag—quite fashionably, I hastened to inform him—dangling from the pit of my arm.

SUSAN MUSGRAVE *has received awards in four different genres—poetry, fiction, creative non-fiction and children's writing—and for her work as an editor. She teaches in* UBC's *Optional-Residency Creative Writing* MFA *program. Her new projects include a novel,* Given, *and a collection of poetry,* Origami Dove, *both to be published in 2011.*

No Longer Just Acting

MARY WALSH

H ere I am, a brassy bit of aging crumpet on the slippery slope side of fifty-five and picking up speed, but because even as a young actress I played an endless series of big, loud, opinionated old bags, it didn't really hit me that I had now become one. I thought I was still just acting. But in a moment of stunning and, frankly, crushing clarity earlier this year, it struck me. I had reached the third stage of womanhood. You know the three stages: young, middle-aged and oh-my-God, Mary, you're looking good. My volume-control button had drifted up on "deafen" there a few years ago, and my internal thermostat got permanently stuck up on "cremate." I'm hot *and* loud now. More like a Caribbean carnival than an actual human being.

And big, well sure, I've always been a big girl for twelve. I'm the size of three regular-sized Canadian actresses. Oh yes, look, if you divide my body into three, see there's room right here for Sheila McCarthy from that *Little Mosque on the*...Zzzzzz...Oh sorry—I don't know what's wrong with me; every time I say the name of that show, I just nod off. And look, there's plenty of room right here for little Cynthia Dale, and we can put her sister Jennifer right there...

And so consequently, of course, I can't find one piece of appropriate clothing to put on my back. I either trot out the door looking for all the world like mutton dressed as lamb or like Great Aunt Mary Magdalene in a shapeless pinny, because, after a certain age, it's impossible to find anything to wear. If you're over a size two—well, over a size ten, really, but still mercifully under a size triple-X—they don't make anything to fit you, and it's getting worse. Yesterday, because I'm blind as a bat in a felt hood because of my encroaching maturity, I ended up in the dressing room of a shop with a size-double-zero dress. Double zero! Where did that come from? I mean, personally I'm still reeling from the time they introduced size zero. Size zero! Size zip. Size nada. Nothing. But now, not even nothing is good enough. We have to shrink ourselves down apparently to size double-nothings.

Oh, never mind feminism and equal pay and all that—sure, now we don't even believe we have a right to take up space in the world anymore. The fellas are over at the gym gulping down steroids, bulking up, and we're here starving ourselves on Diet Coke and Kleenex for roughage while chained to a StairMaster desperately trying to disappear. What's an old dame to do?

And we're still celebrating something called International Women's Day. International Women's *Day?* For God's sake, even root vegetables get a whole week: April 16 to 23 is International Turnip Week. And the entire month of April is National Pecan Month. A whole month for nuts, and women still only get a day.

In my youth, I dreamt of becoming one of those insouciant "roll on, Death, and let's have a go at the angels"-type of old gal, but now, where daily I can almost hear the celestial chorus tuning up for me, well, let's just say I'm not so nonchalant. Now I'm feeling somewhat churlish about the whole thing and kicking deaf heaven with my bootless cries and suffering from the unfairness of it all. Yes I know everybody dies but… *I* have to?

And let's face it, it's not a great time to be an old dame living here in the West, in the centre of our youth-obsessed culture where it's considered a moral failing to look old. But here I am—my bits are collapsing around my knees at the alarming speed of the fall of the former Soviet Union. What am I to do? Because according to the studies, looks still count for everything if you're a woman—and youthful ones at that. With men, it's status, career, money, power and sense of humour, but with women, the only thing that matters is how you look.

Luckily, all this tragic loss, this falling and collapsing—the breasts, the eyelids, the cheeks, the neck, the knees, the arches, the toes (oh, they'd take the dive, too, if they thought there was anywhere to go)—can be solved with just a little cut and paste. Everybody's doing it—snipping out the saggy, droopy bits. Sucking out the surplus. Oh yes, we are daily encouraged to puff up those withered lips with new Allo-Derm. AlloDerm—actual skin that has been harvested from cadavers. Well, that's sure to make anyone more kissable—a big set of blubbery lips stuffed with the dermis of the dead.

While we're on harvesting, isn't that an attractive and comforting idea that they came up with a couple of years ago—the promise that in the future we could each own our own headless organ slave made out of our DNA, ready to be harvested any time we might need a kidney or spare part. Well, can't you just see the whole nightmare scenario played out in front of you from some Japanese horror movie from the fifties. *The Revenge of the Headless Ones.* "No, I will not give you my liver! You give me your head!" All in the pursuit of everlasting youth.

But really, what's so great about being young? Just looking at the poor youngsters breaks your heart... tottering around with their pants down below their bums with their piercings and cuttings and brandings, as if life itself weren't going to cut and pierce and brand them enough. And then the crowd going around dressed up like the bride of Dracula or Morticia or something…Goths. They're into death. God, I love the young. They're so cute. They think you can be into death as if it were a hula hoop or something.

I may be old and deteriorating rapidly, but one thing I'm grateful for: at least I never have to be young again.

MARY WALSH *is a Gemini Award–winning actress and social activist whose inimitable comedy has been a staple of Canadian broadcasting—from* CODCO *and* This Hour Has 22 Minutes *to* Mary Walsh: Open Book *and* Hatching, Matching and Dispatching. *She has appeared in numerous movies, advocated for* OXFAM *and the* CNIB, *and recently hosted a documentary on poverty called* Poor No More.

Face It

LINDA SPALDING

W hat did I do as a child to pass the time? It seemed to go on and on while grown-ups drank highballs and talked in the kitchen... On and on while I made houses out of toothpicks, assembled dreams, looked out the car window at yards and trees. A cat sitting in a window or a dog on a porch. Let's take the old road, my mother would say, and my father would grab the car keys. My brother was ten years older and never part of our ambling drives, which must be why I remember my grandmother with me in the back seat, her presence causing both comfort and pain. Maybe we were inclined to wander during her visits, since she had no car, although I can no more bring back the leisurely pace of those drives than I can bring back my family, all of us being more like a group of negatives than like actual images. Our white faces are dark circles. Our black legs stand in white shoes. What I remember is looking out at the world like a visitor, which is what I was.

Sometimes we took a route through downtown. There may have been the excuse of a stop at the post office, where my father kept a private box for the mail he did not want anyone else to see. Later, my brother had a box in this same post office, where, like our father, he received letters from his various amours. And later still, my own beloved kept a box in a dingy post office in Toronto, where he received letters from me. By then, the days of leisure were past. My brother had his own Cessna, my father had died in the courthouse, and my grandmother, who died a year later, had forgotten who any of us was. The huge petrified log outside the mysterious stone library was there in every season, always the same except for snow or fallen leaves or the wetness of recent rain, but around it everything changed.

Through it all, my mother kept a beautiful house and went to the hairdresser once a week. Catherine Hathaway's beauty shop, located in the front room of her house, consisted of three dryers hunched over three ordinary chairs and a central seat on which curlers were rolled into hair after it was haphazardly cut. In the hallway, the shampoo chair sat across from the open bathroom where the family laundry was stacked. There was nothing glamorous about this place. Catherine's ancient and bowed mother clutched a broom handle and ceaselessly pushed wads of hair across the floor, wearing rolled-down hose and soft slippers. But the lady customers rose from the central chair, after being combed and sprayed, and reached into their pocketbooks. Week after week. Catherine, from a minuscule Missouri town... Catherine, without education or money, bent over and crippled with arthritis, was part of Topeka's elite. This was not because she created beautifully attired marionettes, eggs with whole dioramas inside, feathered boxes, silkscreened fabric, tin flower wreaths, sequined sweaters, painted furniture and beautiful hats. It was because she was central to the life of Topeka. Her shop was its parliament.

I made the mistake of thinking it was a parliament of beauty secrets. Rules, repressions, strictures—how we must model ourselves on the pictures in magazines. In Topeka, no one got a facelift except the governor's mother, who was ·

a friend and a Democrat. And, even so, my mother remarked on it with a mixture of envy and contempt. There were four stages to life and no slipping or sliding between. Age was the great divider, and it was immodest to complain.

Now I'm much older than my mother was then, but women my age have trainers, take yoga and get faces cut and sewn into unnatural shapes. I thought of the parliament. So I made an appointment. It was my little secret. I didn't tell anyone where I was going or that I had come to fear my face. The doctor's suite of rooms was up one flight of marble stairs, with thick carpeting, flocked wallpaper, candles burning at ten in the morning and flowers in a crystal vase. I was greeted by first one and then another and then another young woman, although age was going to be hard to measure here. Had the good doctor applied his skills to his assistants? The three other women in the waiting room were actually girls. I suppose they wanted bigger breasts or fuller lips. I answered the questions on the form I was given. Age... Reason for coming (wasn't it obvious?)... Eventually, I was taken to a room with the usual paper-covered settee, where I sat, waiting to be rescued from myself.

When the doctor came in, I tried to gauge his temper and accomplishment by reading his face, but it was expressionless. I wondered about his age but, again, had no firm idea. He had bangs that hung over his forehead, and he paused every so often to flick them out of his eyes in a boyish way. He asked me to hold a hand mirror up and look at myself. "On the form you state your reason for coming here is baggy eyes."

"Like the saggy baggy elephant in the children's story."

He looked blank.

How could I trust a doctor who had not read the story of the little elephant who doesn't know what he is because he doesn't look like anyone else in the jungle? When a parrot tells him his ears are too big, his nose is too big, and his skin is much, much too big, the little elephant says he'd be glad to improve himself. *But how?* I looked at the hand mirror, wondering the same thing, while the doctor spoke softly about the droop of my lower and upper lids. His surgical method involves a good deal of bleeding and bruising, he said. "Do you have sensitivities?"

The little elephant had tried to smooth out his skin with his trunk. He had soaked in a river with the crocodiles to make his skin shrink. A tiger had offered to take some bites out of his hide.

"I tend to weep."

"With all the cutting, you might end up weeping for the rest of your life," said the doctor blandly. "Or you might never weep again."

I listened to a long litany of risks. If I woke up in the night unable to see, I should go to emergency. I should not call him. This is the end of me—sags, bags, wrinkles, and all, thought the little elephant. And I put on my coat and went down the marble stairs. But as I opened the door to the street, the thought of another door came back to me. I had opened it only a few weeks before.

June Leaf is a sculptor and painter whose work I have loved for years. She and the photographer Robert Frank live and work on Bleeker Street in New York City, where friends may bring up sticks of wood from a pile at the door and sit in front of a tiny fireplace. The two artists are old now, both in their eighties, and live in a hectic jumble of past and present projects. While an acolyte followed Robert from room to room discussing a book project, June poured sherry and talked about Nova Scotia, where they have studios close to the sea. While she talked, I kept peering into the dark corners of the room and then turning to look at her face, whose every line is a gouge where joy and grief are complex sentences. It is a face so expressive that every inch of it speaks.

When she asked me to come with her to pick up a necklace she had taken to be restrung—African beads given to
her by a friend—we went down the dangerous, dingy stairs
and out through the metal door that opens onto the street.
It was this moment that came back to me a few weeks later
in Toronto. I had closed the door behind me as June rushed
down the sidewalk. Then I had followed her, panting. She
was taking great strides and elbowing traffic out of her way
as if we were on an errand of mercy. At the Tibetan shop, she
retrieved the necklace and insisted that I look around. "Isn't
it wonderful? Look at the colours!" For a luxurious moment,
she touched the scarves tenderly. Then we rushed out again
into the night—"Robert may wonder why we are taking so
long"—and up the narrow stairway. The devotion, the love,
the energy all written in her face.

Later, we were led down another set of stairs and into her
studio. Here, the jumble became manic. Lovely things had
been flung to the ground. "I don't like that. Leave it there."
Metal angels clung to paintings; tiny ladders climbed into
emptiness; a reconstructed sewing machine kept painted figures dancing in circles. June moved among her creations like
a divinity. She is a tall woman, and the face, with its history,
is intent. Her strong hands fastened a tiny figure to a tipping
metal stair with a kind of benevolence, then fired up her soldering iron.

"Your face," she said, staring hard, "is changed from the
last time we met."

Oh dear. I'd better hide in a dark place where my bags and
sags and creases and wrinkles won't show, thought the little
elephant. And he ran into a cave where it was dark.

"I've got... well... older."

"Before it looked out. But now it looks *in*."

June made this statement with apparent approval, but
what did she mean? In the big mirror over the messy vanity

in Catherine Hathaway's beauty shop, I had always avoided my face and looked at the reflection of Catherine, who stood behind me, comb in hand. She had taught me to make a papier mâché marionette. Yellow hair, a huge nose and a silly voice. Madame Elephant. She had taught me to make jewellery and costumes and to write a script. How did Catherine create such amazing things with her arthritic hands? How did any of the women in that place do what they did—my mother outlasting the pain of my father's sudden death, then, years later, celebrating her eightieth birthday with such grace the year my brother crashed his plane? And why does a look in the mirror now show me the face of my grandmother, whose presence beside me in the back seat caused me to ponder time and death? How many Christmases would I have with her? Or with my mother? Or anyone else? Life was going to be loss after loss and then extinction. What sense did it make? The dancers to spin. The stairs to be climbed. And now time is moving so much faster.

But when I look, I see a world I helped make. I've grown my bounty of sins. But also beauty, adjustment, understanding and triumph. I hold tight to my soldering iron. Because, when the little elephant trumpets his fear of the dark and looks out of the cave, he sees a circle of big, baggy elephants— all very beautiful—and he finally knows what he is.

LINDA SPALDING *is the author of three novels,* Daughters of Captain Cook, The Paper Wife, *and* Mere, *co-written with her daughter Esta. Her non-fiction work includes* The Follow, *shortlisted for the Trillium Book Award and the Pearson Writers' Trust Non-Fiction Prize, and* Who Named the Knife. *An editor of* Brick, *she has received the Harbourfront Festival Prize for her contribution to the Canadian literary community.*

Rust

LYNN MILES

Every line in your face is a road you've been down
It's a freight train you hopped, a night in a strange town
It's a joke that you told, a tear that rolled on
It's a sad story you heard, or a lover who's gone

And the scars on your hands, that's the hard work
    that you've done
It's the skin that you've touched, all the little wars
    that you've won
It's the baby you cradled, it's the letters you wrote
It's that time you held on, it's that time you let go

And the footprints you leave are perfect and deep
And your soul is a place that is tough and it's sweet
And the shadow you cast is straight and it's true
But the lines and the scars are what I love about you

And the rust in your voice, that's the dust and the rain
It is the choices defended again and again and again
It's the life that you've lived, it's the friends come and gone
It's the highways and the truck stops and the cold
    grey dawn

LYNN MILES *is a Juno Award–winning Canadian singer, songwriter and producer. Her* Love Sweet Love *was chosen as* Album of the Year *by* Penguin Eggs *magazine, and her music has been lauded in* Billboard *and the* New York Times, *among others. She has record deals in Canada, the* USA *and Europe and is probably touring as you read this.*

Connecting (Feminist) Lines

DIANA MAJURY

....

Feminism, to me, is a complicated but compelling means of understanding and responding to the inequitable world in which we live. It offers us long lists of things we should and shouldn't do, accompanied by extensive feminist critiques of the lists, or of even having lists in the first place. (No wonder the movement is seen by many as way too prescriptive. Really: who needs another bossy voice in your life telling you how to look, dress and comport yourself? Why would we simply replace one set of rules with another?)

Yet I'm a feminist and a list person—which makes the feminist lists easy for me. I can choose to adopt or reject the prescriptions, but they make me think—about who I am and who I want to be in the world, what it really means to try to live what I believe, and how to apply to myself and my daily life the ideas that I regularly spout to and about others.

Like many feminists, I think women have been sucked into being ultra critical of our bodies and their parts such that most of us are out of touch with our physical selves. We worry about not measuring up, about "fixing" our hair, our clothes, our selves. I love that feminism challenges this devaluation of women, this notion that we should be judged in the narrowest of terms—our physical attractiveness. I love that it pushes us to be more self-accepting, to reject expectations that make us unhappy.

Feminism reminds us that beauty should not be defined in terms of youth or body type, faces or noses, legs or breasts, skin or hair colour. We're supposed to love each other and ourselves for who we are, however we appear. But it's not so easy. As feminists we've had huge debates over makeup, hair dye, cosmetic surgery, high heels and showing cleavage. We certainly don't all agree, and many of us break even the rules we do agree on. Contradictions abound. We're hard on ourselves and on each other.

I'm a lesbian, so for me the list is even longer and more fraught. The plaid-shirt-and-work-boots look of the '70s was a very limiting stereotype, but it also allowed us to recognize each other and feel solidarity. For many lesbians, it was a big loss moving on from "dyke attire." And the internal lesbian critiques are sometimes even harsher than the feminist ones. We accuse each other and ourselves of being too femme, of buying into gendered stereotypes, of trying to "pass."

According to my rule book, embracing feminism and lesbianism means embracing my own aging. Aging itself is part of life's process; we shouldn't try to hide or disguise it, bemoan it or decry it.

But, again, not so easy. The image of the old woman in our culture is not one of beauty. And there's an undercurrent of censure—even among feminists—of women who fail to take care of themselves as they age, who "let themselves go." Aging is a drag, and women who are obviously not young either are seen as past their time or are simply not seen. They're hidden, and they hide, away. As older women, we're complimented when told we *don't* look our age; we're encouraged to "be as young as we feel" and to deny our aging with hair dye, skin creams and surgery.

I have struggled to live up to what I see as an important feminist goal: to refuse to aspire to traditional notions of female beauty; to be content with the body I have; and to engage in minimal lifestyle and body adjustments in the pursuit of an elusive, other, more physically beautiful me. I think I've been moderately successful, although others' response— to both the goal and its achievement—will no doubt range from shock at my rigid application of the "rules" to amusement at my delusion that I have in any way challenged the heterosexist and sexist norms of beauty!

I don't wear makeup of any kind. (Never any good at putting it on, I tended towards a heavy hand that gave me a Vampira kind of look. I doubt this ever made me more attractive by anyone's standards.) I do worry about my weight, but I'm very hard on myself for doing so. I love to eat and drink, so when I've gone overboard, I describe my curtailment of the above as "being sensible," never as a diet; dieting is not feminist.

I don't shave my legs or my armpits. This is a tough one because I have a lot of body hair. But I actually like my body hair, especially the hair under my arms. I think it's sexy. I was even taken with the idea of entering the Michigan Womyn's Music Festival hairiest armpits contest—until I surveyed the competition and had to concede I was a lightweight in the armpit hair department—clearly an indication of how little female armpit hair is normally on display.

I hated shaving, nicking, the stubble. It's incomprehensible to me why *not* shaving never caught on. And yet I'm very self-conscious of my hairy legs. They do get stares, and I read the stares as horror and disgust. Children tell me, "You have legs like a man," and I cringe. As a result, I almost never show my naked legs. I don't wear skirts or dresses (made easier by having subscribed to the lesbian anti-skirt rule!), nor shorts. And I put on a bathing suit only if I have to and only among friends. So I cover up my rebellion and ask myself, Is a hidden principle really a principle? Perhaps a closet non-shaver is not challenging… anything.

I don't wear a bra, either. And I have to say I feel a bit abandoned by my generation of feminists, many of whom embraced bralessness in the early days but now, with sagging breasts and tight-fitting clothes, have reneged.

I'm told bra burning never actually happened, but in my mind it did. I imagine a raging bonfire surrounded by hundreds of daring women stripping off their shirts, unclasping their cumbersome breast containers and flinging them into the flames with a whoop. How liberating! What fun! Instead, bra burning has somehow become synonymous with feminist extremism or foolishness.

I continue to think the bra is oppressive and, for many of us, unnecessary. I have small breasts, and that makes going without a bra much easier. Then again, to my huge discomfort, my nipples feel the cold and stand out at the slightest encouragement, so being braless is sometimes a struggle for me, too. Mostly I opt for loose tops or jackets. So in a way I am closeted here, too.

I was doing okay on the aging front until recently. My hair, which was dark, has been mostly grey for some time, and I like it. The grey came in salt and pepper—in the going-grey norms, I greyed nicely. I had never dyed my hair and am not tempted to do so now, although I'm sure that it makes me look older than my feminist peers, most of whom *do* dye their hair. Who knows what someone is reacting to when they offer you a senior's discount or call you dearie? I think it's my grey hair, but it could be other signs of aging. When age spots began to appear on my face, I saw them as blemishes, as hugely visible negative markers. But now I've almost developed a fondness for them.

As a kid, I had lots of freckles, but my red-headed best friend, Ruthie Baker, had even more. She won the local freckle contest, and I came second. (No doubt this early participation in competition as a means of celebrating "undesirable" body bits made the armpit hair competition familiar and appealing. But acceptance through competition may be a suspect strategy; competition is on my feminist "no" list.) Because I loved Ruthie's freckles, I came to love my own. And now I see my brown aging spots as my freckles returning— bigger and better—full circle to my youth, reconnecting me with a long-lost childhood friend. Age spots as freckles grown old? I know I am engaging in feminist mythologizing, trying to make aging easier to accept. But the myth works for me. I feel connected to Ruthie through my age spots.

It is the lines in my face that I have the most trouble with. I stare at my facial furrows, the banks of flesh curling around them. The lines are many, and they are in the wrong places— not attractively situated at all. Some are deep and uneven; some superficial and characterless. They look dry and thirsty. I have been quite unhappy with these lines. They make me look old.

And yet the other day I had a wrinkle revelation. At a long and tedious meeting, I looked over at my friend, a feminist, who is my age. Like me, she is grey haired and makeup-less (although she does wear a bra). Bored with the meeting, I fixated on my friend's face. She has lots of lines. And these lines moved as she talked, they opened when she laughed, bulged out when she was unhappy, scrunched up when she was uncertain and rested attentively when she listened. I looked at her lines, and I loved them—they were signs of wisdom, life and learning; they were guides to her responses and emotions. They were entrancing. I stared at her for the rest of the meeting, interpreting its tone and outcomes through the lines on my dear friend's face. I enjoyed myself immensely and saw her—as I always have—as extremely beautiful. What was new was noticing her lines and seeing them as part of her beauty, not as detracting from it.

That evening when I looked in the mirror, I was shocked by how similar the lines in my face—the lines I so disliked—were to the lines I loved in my friend's face. The likeness was unbelievable: the same folds, and curls and banks that in her I had read as deep and rich in meaning and emotion, I had seen as static, empty and ugly in myself. But, like Ruthie's freckles, the lines are a bond, a commonality, a connection. I can't yet say I love my own wrinkles, but I do see them differently, more positively. I smile at the thought of others reading me through their shifting movements.

So in the end, I am what I am—an aging feminist. It is my feminism—with its lists and dictates, its hope and acceptance, its recognition that women are beautiful in multiple and varied ways—that gently encourages me to welcome my aging self. Although initially I resist and feel bad about each new sign as it comes, I have slowly come to accept, even to embrace, the markers of my age that bond me with my peers. Unlike my hairy legs and my braless breasts, I am not hiding my aging, and I like that. And maybe as an old woman I will grow into the overtly rebellious, convention-flouting feminist I am in my heart.

DIANA MAJURY *grew up in Winnipeg and is growing old in Ottawa. She teaches in the law department at Carleton University, focusing primarily on human rights and equality. She has been active as a feminist all of her adult life, championing issues relating to violence against women, women's health and Charter equality matters.*

Seeing

Levity in the Face of Gravity

RENATE MOHR

In this narrative, the protagonist is a fifty-five-year-old woman who has been invited to contribute to a collection of essays celebrating aging—let's call it an uplifting, thoughtful, Canadian version of Nora Ephron's book *I Feel Bad about My Neck*. The protagonist is delighted and accepts immediately. She figures because she's one of very few women who actually embraces birthdays and likes her body, this will be a cakewalk. That, plus she's desperate for a release from the novel she's been working on for the last three years. She figures she'll write about the triumph of the human spirit (because that's what all good novels, films and fairy tales are about). Her life fits this outline perfectly. She had breast cancer at age forty-three and, after two mastectomies, had to relearn to like her body (a triumph!). A few years later, she quit her day job with tenure and benefits to write full-time for nothing (another triumph!). Now, at age fifty-five, she's in the process of moving four hundred kilometres away from her partner and dog into a small loft on the Toronto Islands in order to finish the aforementioned novel (a triumph in progress!). It's a cakewalk, indeed. All she needs is a beginning, a middle and an end.

Not wanting to appear too arrogant about how easy this task will be, she decides to do some research, so on the day she leaves Ottawa (in a little white Honda, packed with beeswax candles and enough clothes and books to last her for three months), she stops in at a mall to buy a copy of Nora Ephron's book. As she steps out of the car, she is strong (strong), she is invincible (invincible), she is Helen, ready to conquer.

In the bookstore, she scans the shelves but doesn't find Ephron, so waits behind the attractive man with greying temples who is being served by the only clerk, a young man with a dark mole on his left cheek, who is curiously unaffected by the line that is growing behind her and snaking around tables of discounted books. Finally she is next in line. She resists the urge to straighten the horn-rimmed glasses perched precariously on his nose and instead asks him if he has a copy of Nora Ephron's most recent book. Something on his cuff diverts his attention, so she repeats the question. He looks up, rolls his eyes and in slow motion steps sideways to the computer.

"What's the name?"

"Ephron, Nora Ephron."

"E-F-R-O-N," he speaks as he types.

"Sorry, it's E-P-H-R-O-N." She wonders why she apologizes (especially given that she is invincible) and tells herself it must be because she's feeling bad about the glasses that she didn't straighten and that now look worse on him than before.

The clerk picks at his mole and once again rolls his eyes at the computer as if she's purposely chosen a more difficult spelling. She senses an impatient shuffling behind her and wonders why this is taking so long.

Finally he looks up and out of his meek little mouth comes a roar that stills the room. "You want *I Feel Bad about My Neck and Other Thoughts on Being a Woman?*"

Her hand shoots up to cover the nakedness above her collarbones. She glances back at the line, because the humiliation is not complete until she can count the number of faces staring at her. Seven.

"Yes," she answers quietly and discreetly drops her hand to her side.

"We have one copy left," he tells her with the smile of a snake making a gift of an apple, his eyes unabashedly counting the rings on her neck, as he would those of a cross-sectioned oak. She resists the urge to remove his precious horn-rimmed glasses and grind them under the heel of her sturdy red boot.

Safely seated in her little Honda, she checks out her neck in the rear-view mirror (something, by the way, Ephron suggests one should never do because rear-view mirrors are never flattering, but the protagonist hasn't read the book yet, so it's an honest mistake), and it suddenly occurs to her that her reaction is that of a stranger. Not that she's never noticed the changes to her aging body but, rather, that she's rarely been bothered by them. She's never complained about menopause (it pales in comparison with chemo) nor drooping breasts (because she has none), and she's learned to celebrate the tall, thin build that, on good days, makes boyish sexy (an attitude that could well be considered a triumph!). She has accepted wrinkles, like birthdays, as evidence that she is alive (absolutely a triumph!), and for that, she is generally grateful. That was the whole point of agreeing to write the positive narrative on aging, she thinks as she carefully studies the reflection, which highlights not only the lines on her neck but the looseness of the skin, neither of which fits well into her tight story outline.

That's the beginning.

To get from the beginning to the middle, we'll have to skip to the part where the protagonist is living in her loft on Algonquin Island, a twelve-minute ferry ride from downtown

Toronto. To help with the transition, this might be a good time to take a sip of tea, close your eyes and picture her, once again invincible (because she is actually making some headway on the novel—chapters of which are spread across her kitchen table, on the spiral steps up to the bedroom and on most every level surface there is). Picture her getting off the ferry, taking the subway to Queen Street, and walking west to meet a friend at a vegetarian restaurant for dinner. She checks her phone and slows her pace so that she's not unfashionably early. Signs on storefronts advertise everything from buttons to used furniture.

A petite, dark-haired woman stands in the middle of the sidewalk stirring cream in a tiny white cauldron cradled in her cupped hand. She is a Natalie Portman look-alike. The same dark eyes, the same sexy mouth and the same perfect neck. She stops the protagonist, first with her eyes, then with a light grip on her arm.

The protagonist is bewitched by the young beauty.

"I think I have something you are needing, and if you have a moment, I will demonstrate it for you." The woman holds up the little pot with a reverence generally associated with the offering of holy wine and smiles a beatific smile.

The protagonist hesitates, trying to place the accent. The petite woman with the perfectly fitted neck takes this as a yes and, pulling her by the elbow, guides her into a store the size of a modest walk-in closet. Miniature white pots with gold lettering line glass shelves that are lit from below. With lightning speed, the protagonist realizes this shop sells creams and cosmetics. Unfortunately, it's too late to run.

"Please, you must sit." Manicured fingers wave the protagonist onto a white bar stool. "You must excuse my English."

The protagonist removes her inelegant knapsack, takes the assigned seat and asks, "Where are you from?" (because, truth be told, she is far more interested in learning about this mysterious creature's life than in hearing her pitch).

"Israel."

"Ah." The protagonist smiles at this rare opportunity to show off her few words of Hebrew. *"Erev tov!"*

Suddenly, an accordion arm unfolds and a round mirror appears in front of the protagonist's face. The saleswoman flips the mirror to the dreaded magnified side on which pores are craters and lines are canyons.

Any hopes of discussing Middle East politics are dashed.

As if the reflection itself were not bad enough, the young beauty places her fingertips on the skin under the protagonist's eyes and pulls her cheeks earthward.

"You see?!" she exclaims with the enthusiasm of an explorer (of craters and canyons). "Your face, he is very, very dry and very, very thirsty and he is pulling down." At this point in the discovery, she frowns. "Look how much he is dropping."

She shakes her head and presses into the loose flesh.

Quick as a mood swing, the woman's expression changes, and she lifts the miniature holy grail (that still sits in her palm) towards the light on the mirror. "It's true he's very dry and he will keep pulling down and pulling down, but—the vitamins in the cream will help him to breathe!"

The protagonist can't help but smile. Just a moment ago she had thought his condition was terminal.

"I will show you how the magic will work for him. I will work only on the left side so you can see the difference." She delicately touches the stir stick with cream onto the left cheek and massages the folds around the eye. The protagonist is relieved and closes her eyes because she can no longer bear witness to his haunting decline. She listens in darkness as the dire consequences of not following a strict regimen (which has now grown to three different creams daily) are outlined.

Finally the lecture and the massage come to an end.

"Look how beautiful he looks now!"

The protagonist opens her eyes and a finger is pointing to the left side of her face.

"See!" Unnaturally white teeth flash a broad eureka smile.

The protagonist leans into the mirror, but it doesn't help. There is a sensation of tightness around her eye and cheek, but she cannot tell the difference between the dying side and the resurrected side. He, as a whole, still looks terminal.

Thinking of the conflict in the Middle East and of how relatively privileged her life has been, the protagonist smiles and says, "Yes, of course I see."

The large brown eyes fixed on hers well with pleasure.

A glance at her blessed phone becomes the opportunity to escape the chair. "I'm sorry, I'm late for an appointment." As she slides off the faux leather, the sales pitch flies into high gear. She's offered the creams, in a just-this-one-time-deal, at a price that resembles the cost of a one-way airplane ticket to Tel Aviv.

"No, thank you, but I don't have that kind of money."

"I'll tell you what—we can throw in a free facial, just for you, just this time."

The protagonist gracefully declines.

Natalie Portman hands her a shiny card with gold flourishes. "If you change your mind." She shakes her head, looks at the little pot in her hand and then gently taps a cheek. "It's too bad. He could be so much better."

The protagonist slings on her knapsack and, feeling considerably less strong and less invincible, hurries over to the vegetarian restaurant.

Breathlessly she apologizes to her friend. She sits at the table and leans her face forward (doing nothing to give away the fact that his left side is his good side).

"One side of my face looks better. Which is it?"

The friend, patient and honest, takes her time and finally nods.

"The right side!"

Although the protagonist laughs as she recounts the experience over a large bowl of Moroccan stew, later on in the evening, as she makes her way back to the ferry terminal, she catches her reflection in a store window, and although she can't see him well, she knows he is pulling down, he is thirsty and he is sad, and tragically, he's only going to get worse with age.

If there is one sip of tea left, now is the time. The beginning and middle have led us to the end.

As the ferry makes its way across the channel, she stands on the deck in the October air and contemplates a time in the future when he is so droopy and sad that no one loves him any more and all that is left for the protagonist is to throw herself into the dark waters of Toronto Harbour (with stones in her pockets, because she is, after all, a writer).

"Hi!" A little girl with long, dark curls dances across the ferry deck. Her blouse is impossibly white, and her blue floor-length tunic flutters as she twirls. There are bows on her shoes, and she moves with the grace and charm of a ten-year-old whose beauty is unassailable.

"Did you see them?" she asks. A little hand points over the boat rail.

Three white swans swim side by side in a perfect swath of light beamed down by a full moon.

"No, I didn't." The protagonist is enchanted. "Are you a dancer?" she asks, pointing to the patent leather shoes, hoping to keep her visitor close by.

The little girl laughs as if she's been asked an insanely stupid question. "No!" She slaps her side and laughs some more.

"I'm a singer in the Children's Opera Company, and we just did a concert with a children's choir from Kenya!"

"How did it go?"

"Awesome." She completes a pirouette and then leans in closer to the protagonist, as if about to share a confidence. "You know what's funny?" she asks. "In the winter, when you've got your boots on and you try sliding on the ice but it's all bumpy and sticky and, no matter how hard you try, you can't slide—but then you walk on a path and *swoosh*—you go sliding when you don't even expect it!" She throws her head back, filling the night air with starbursts of laughter. Before the protagonist can respond, the bows on the shoes have disappeared into a gathering of passengers preparing to disembark.

The protagonist smiles.

It's only after the third magi disappears that she recognizes the gift.

A beginning, a middle and an end (and *swoosh*, the triumph of the human spirit).

....

RENATE MOHR *returned home to Ottawa. In spite of the effects of gravity on her face (still affectionately known as* him*), her significant others (people and dog) welcomed her back. As the recipient of numerous awards for short fiction, she thought writing a novel would be a cakewalk. This is the first time she has ever been wrong about anything.*

Ways of Seeing

MERI COLLIER

I've been drawing for a long time now, but I still remember my first class in the 1960s. To my eighteen-year-old eyes, the painfully thin model appeared old and haggard. After the class, a few of us wondered how they expected us to draw such an unattractive person.

I view the models I draw in a different light now. Things that I see as signs of aging are mildly disturbing but surprisingly interesting and richer in contours, the skin more eloquent with details.

I admire the confidence that allows mature models to disrobe before a group of people. I see them and acknowledge the changes in my own body.

Sometimes, looking in the mirror after my morning shower, I notice the skin on the underside of my arm—*my mother's arm*, so familiar, now my arm! I wonder with amazement how or when it became that way; I am surprised it has appeared so suddenly. And in my next breath, I accept it as part of my own aging process.

It is nothing I had anticipated, but it's here, and it doesn't really mean much beyond the fact that I've been around for sixty-four years. I bring my arm down to my side out of my sightline, and the thought vanishes with it.

Bodies are full of surprises, and each one is individual, yet I often try to draw what I think I know, rather than what is actually before me.

Mature bodies are particularly challenging because they're usually hidden, not displayed publicly. The visual vocabulary is not so familiar. My challenge is to look, see and believe what is in front of me. I derive pleasure as I explore and learn.

Had I looked more closely at my first model, I might have seen what was there, not what was missing: the distribution of weight, the centre of gravity, the way the flesh flows from the bone, the uniqueness of the person before me...

I continue to find older subjects a challenge to draw. I concentrate and learn and discover new things.

I find my older body a challenge too—demanding attention, learning and discovery.

MERI COLLIER *trained at the Ontario College of Art and Design in material arts and has worked in oil painting, pottery and photography. Her interest in the human body materializes in loose, spontaneous impressions. She is currently searching out trapeze artists and circus arts as subject matter. Recent detours have taken her to experimenting in watercolour and landscapes in Greece, Spain and Italy.*

Ghosts

SUSAN LIGHTSTONE

In retrospect, that December afternoon had a clear Dickensian feel to it. Like a serialized novel, the hours unfolded, revealing a series of small chapters, each building on the one that preceded it. And just as Dickens's works were personal attempts to come to terms with his harsh, mean childhood, my own serial was an effort to come to terms with where I now fit in the world.

Here's what happened. That afternoon, I was at work. It had been a particularly busy day, as I closed up the office for the holidays and tied up a lot of messy loose ends. I was still working full-time at age fifty-four. After an unexpected divorce three years earlier, I knew retirement would be very, very far in my future. I'd been invited for an early-afternoon holiday tea party at the home of a former neighbour, but I lost track of the hours, and by the time I looked at my watch, it was mid-afternoon. I arrived at the party as it was starting to drift to its natural end, a couple of early birds already pulling on their boots and coats to leave.

I was grateful to be invited. After my divorce, I left the neighbourhood—the place we'd raised our children—for an apartment building several streets away. It's awfully easy to forget someone once she's left her immediate vicinity—and left under circumstances that make a lot of fifty-something women nervous. It's a dangerous time for women my age. Kids are launching, nests are emptying—and many long-time married couples are realizing they no longer have much in common. The love they once shared has become a diminished nub of "just getting along." Although both parties might want out of a floundering marriage, no thoughtful, aging woman does it casually. We all know the stats. Divorce is hard on men and women, but "moving on" for women of a certain age looks different (and often a lot lonelier) than it does for men of that vintage.

I was struck when I entered the living room by how all the women sitting, sipping their tea, seemed to have aged so significantly. Then I realized I probably looked a good couple of years older too. I hadn't seen most of them for at least that long. The years between fifty and sixty can be hard on anybody's face, no matter how splendid life's agenda. Until I left the neighbourhood, I was seeing these women on a regular basis—out walking the dog, shopping or dropping kids off at school. Age creeps up imperceptibly day by day, but give it a couple of years and it's amazing what accumulates!

I started making the rounds, teacup and shortbread in hand, talking to each in turn. Everyone's kids seemed okay—some better than others, but more or less launched. As with any talk about one's children, a grain of salt is always necessary. The edited version is delivered to mere acquaintances; the real dirt (job loss, school failure, messy breakups, etc.) is reserved for true friends. As for the women themselves, most were retired, and none seemed particularly passionate about anything. "Flat" is the word that wandered in and sat in my mind as I listened to the soft voices conversing around the room.

When the entire gang started exchanging stories of their experiences with plantar fasciitis and the sorry state of their feet, I felt a chill come over me. I've got to get the hell out of here, I thought. It was more than mere boredom; I'd felt the cold touch of recognition of a life I'd been forced by circumstance to change.

I wondered: How did that happen to those women? Did I used to be like that? I shivered as I drove away, en route to my afternoon errands. I'd had an eerie and telling glimpse of my former self at that party. Maybe a spirit had been sent to remind me that having to worry about keeping a roof over my head might actually be a good thing.

And then I was out of the shadowy realm of "what might have been" and into the bright blast of Loblaws, shopping list in hand. Nothing like a here-and-now task to shake off the past-life phantoms in one's path. Poking through the bread choices, I heard a familiar voice call my name. A former work colleague—a woman my age who had split with her long-term first husband around the same time I had. I hadn't seen her for a year or so. And she looked fabulous. Radiant, in fact.

She couldn't wait to talk to me. Remember when we last spoke, she asked. I did remember. She'd told me about this handsome musician in Montreal she was interested in, but he had yet to notice her. At the time, I'd thought she might be a bit crackers imagining she would land this fellow, given her age and situation. "Well, he's here, he's in this very store, and he's with me now." Sure enough, up wandered this charming man, obviously smitten with my pal.

And there I was, having recently begun a relationship with my own wonderful new man. There's nothing like being handed the opportunity to have another chance and seizing it. We talked, the three of us, standing amidst baguettes and buns, about how awful situations can yield up great possibilities. How love reappears in new guises. I quoted Louis Pasteur: "Chance favours the prepared mind." Maybe we were all ready to keep growing up. Maybe we had grown out of our previous relationships. We laughed at the randomness of life, and I told them how I had met my new beau at a New Year's Eve party—the sort of party I'd detested in my previous life, dismissed as frivolous and silly.

We mused about how freeing it is to be out of the constraints that had bound us for so long. How one can rethink and reinvent oneself in chapter two. It's breathtaking and frightening. I realize, as I digest the day later, I'd been touched again, but this time by my "now"—a warmer, livelier spirit than my past.

We parted and I headed to the dairy section, where I bumped into my friend Liz. I've known her for nearly thirty years. She is kind, reliable and good. And she was content with her life, which included interesting work, a loving husband and three great kids. A strong foundation she carefully considered and regularly tended. Over the years, I've watched her manage the unexpected hardships life randomly hands us. She is always calm, pragmatic and stalwart. I admire her. That day, we meandered through the store, chatting, comparing notes and figuring out when we were going to get together.

As Liz and I stood together in the checkout line, a former neighbour came up and began speaking to us. This is when the day's events turned worrisome. The busy-ness of the checkout line is not the place to start a serious conversation, but that's what happened. Our former neighbour launched into a soliloquy. She and her husband finally split, ending a long-troubled marriage. She was now living on her own in an apartment, and it was awful. But she'd heard that I had a new man in my life, and she congratulated me on that.

It was all too much for me to take in and respond to in any cogent, helpful manner. I did get out a few sentences about "a man" not being life's goal; rather, the objective is to sort out oneself and move forward. The real work after divorce is not finding a replacement but focusing on redefining oneself. Blah, blah, blah... I think I sounded like a lightweight Dr. Phil (and he's already a lightweight). Plus, I felt hypocritical, given how I was enjoying my second chance, with a man along for the ride. Then the checkout line took over, rolling Liz and me away from the woman. I went back to where she was standing, hugged her and told her to call me for coffee. She needed support; I hoped she would get it and be able to move on. I remembered. I was in her shoes not so long ago.

As I packed my groceries into my car, the afternoon started to make sense, taking on its serial form. I realized I'd been visited by the same three ghosts Dickens sent to visit that old misanthrope, Ebenezer Scrooge—Christmases Past, Present and Yet to Come. But, unlike Scrooge, I was awake during the entire process.

The incident in the checkout line was my glimpse into the future and the most unsettling of the trio of visitations. This spirit was more tentative, less fully resolved than the others, telling me my future is shakier than my past and present. I compare Liz with our floundering former neighbour, realizing my work can never stop. I want to be as sorted out and as solid as Liz, prepared for whatever random events will come my way. Ready to be self-sufficient. Ready to be alone. I'm not finished. I need to listen to the advice I gave to my distraught neighbour. I must constantly refine and redefine myself. From here on, this will be my work.

I don't know if, like Ebenezer, I was redeemed at the end of that afternoon. I was, however, left with a vivid sense that I'm satisfied with my life as it's currently rolling out and how I'm growing up and into it. As for the future, who knows? In the meantime, I'm headed in the right direction. My ghosts told me so.

....

SUSAN LIGHTSTONE *is a mother by choice, a sister by chance, a lawyer by profession and a writer by calling. She lives in Ottawa but spends many days on the road, working and exploring the world.*

My Grandmothers' Skin

VAL NAPOLEON

Far from anywhere, the tricksters from all around the world keep a private lounge. It is a place where they can relax, chew the fat, and tell war stories about their various antics and fantastic doings. The decor is luxuriant with the rich textures of rare woods and fine fabrics of red, purple and gold. Enormous plants spread bright, leafy canopies over fat easy chairs upholstered in dark brown leather. In the background, you can hear the tinkling of fountains and snatches of big band music.

Some describe the trickster as an intellectual instrument for indigenous peoples around the world—a way of dealing with that which is bizarre, contradictory or a little crazy. Others describe the trickster as a deeply flawed but divine figure that symbolizes the frailty of humans and gods. Although humans may not agree on the matter, the air of the lounge is filled with boisterous voices and much laughter and knee slapping.

The sky-goddess tricksters take up one end of the lounge. These are the mysterious Tibetan khandromas who ride the clouds and rainbows and storms and whose specialty is messing with the weather and with heroes. The air around them feels charged and sparkles with little rainbows and brilliant ice crystals. Sometimes they help heroes too; it just depends. Right now they are kicking back and telling jokes.

Tarantula, Bobtail Rabbit, Mink, Weget, Nanabush, Wisakedjak and Coyote sit among the many others elsewhere in the room. In one corner watching Warner Brothers reruns are Wile E. Coyote and Bugs Bunny. The older tricksters despise these new "Hollywood tricksters." "Compared with us," the oldsters grumble, "They are not authentic, and they lack imagination. Those guys just haven't developed beyond the one-dimensional characters they started out as." They shake their trickster heads. But this doesn't bother Wile E. Coyote and Bugs Bunny. "Those complainers are just jealous because we are more famous," they think, contentedly slurping their Shirley Temples.

The collective indigenous feminist consciousness that is emerging and re-emerging around the world has produced some new tricksters. One of these is called Headache. She is sassy and menopausal and is greatly amused by the headaches she can render—just by asking difficult questions. Headache's specialty is to slap people upside the head when they get too full of themselves.

When Headache pulls up a chair to join Weget, Nanabush and Wisakedjak, they roll their eyes and try to ignore her. They have not appreciated Headache's efforts to introduce a feminist perspective to the trickster world. They are also suspicious of Headache's trickster credentials. Secretly, she wishes that Weget, Nanabush and Wisakedjak would experience a couple of really good hot flashes—that would sure level them out and take off those arrogant edges. She imagines each of them breaking out into a humdinger—red-faced and panting, with rivers of sweat running down their faces and their bodies. But she keeps these little thoughts to herself. Since she loves the discomfort of others, Headache orders a scotch on the rocks and sits back, smiling. Weget, Nanabush and Wisaked-jak realize that she is not leaving, so before long they are deep into planning possible antics for the coming year.

The next day, nursing a slight hangover, Headache stretches out on the couch and returns to a recent preoccupation with the various physical manifestations of aging. Last week, while trying to firm up her stubborn underarm sags by some weight lifting, she caught sight of the back of her arm in the mirror. Even the skin above the elbow was drooping—her elbows, for Pete's sake! The endless hot flashes are bad enough, but to have her elbows droop?!

She picks up a copy of O magazine and, flipping through it, is arrested by a two-page spread of the "aging" Lauren Hutton, a former supermodel. Hutton is a knockout—slender and blonde, with great teeth that are very white. Her skin positively glows, and her face has only a few beautiful lines—and in the most becoming places. She is introduced as having "made authenticity, audacity, and ease her fashion watchwords—and forged a new freedom for women. And she is still at it." She looks like she is having a lot of fun cavorting across the pages. Headache wonders whether Hutton is some kind of trickster created by the lucrative quest-for-youth industry. "Could be," Headache muses aloud, "One mean-ass trickster up to no end of mischief in the life of the average woman."

A few pages further on, Headache pauses at a L'Oréal advertisement for a product called Revitalift that asks the reader whether she wants to "stop deep-set eye wrinkles." The ad claims that it will "repair," "restore" and "protect." Like Lauren Hutton, the woman featured in the ad is also aging gorgeously with utterly charming little laugh lines and dainty crows' feet. "Yeah right," observes Headache, " 'Because you're worth it.' I have eagles' feet around my eyes. I doubt even Revitalift could do that kind of heavy lifting."

Headache drops the magazine, suddenly tired of living in an anti-wrinkle world where the hard-earned record of a life is devalued into little more than a form of damage that needs to be repaired. She has her share of wrinkles, complete with the standard body sags. Her hair is grey and unruly, and she needs orthopaedic inserts because even her arches are losing the fight with gravity. She sighs deeply and wonders when the beauty of wrinkles was lost. Sitting up, she decides to explore this little question, and since her research methodology is eavesdropping, she drops in on Val and Karen.

Val is talking about wrinkles: "When I was very little, I loved my grandmothers' skin. One grandmother was Cree, the other English. Their skin was finely wrinkled and wonderfully soft. I would sit beside them and touch their skin just to feel the softness of the wrinkles. I thought their skin was absolutely beautiful, and I would stroke their arms or hands, and sometimes their faces too. I marvelled at the networks of delicate lines and folds. Eventually, of course, they would get sick of me and slap me away. But as soon as they sat back down, I would sidle over to sit with them again. I couldn't help myself. I thought they were exquisitely beautiful because of their wrinkles."

"What would a child think today?" Karen wonders. "With all the hype about cosmetic surgery and facelifts, could she think wrinkles are beautiful? Or would she just see them as old skin that is damaged?"

"I don't know." Val is pulling a little at the skin that is loosening on her neck. "It is my neck that is getting old. I saw a book title somewhere about a woman who felt bad about her neck. Imagine, writing a book about your neck. Maybe we should have a look at that."

Headache travels on to eavesdrop on Ruth and Mary, who are exchanging hot-flash stories.

Ruth is complaining: "There I am at the front of the class having these almost overwhelming hot flashes. Sweat starts pouring down my face, and I feel it running down my whole body. I keep talking like nothing is happening. It wasn't like the students couldn't notice, though. A couple of times, I even wondered what I was talking about."

"Oh, that's nothing," Mary responds, "I had a hot flash in a sweat lodge at home last week. When the heat from inside my body met the heat outside my body, I thought I was going to explode. I had nowhere to go! I was just gasping! But I had to be quiet, you know, so I could be private about it."

"That's like having a hot flash when it's really, really hot, like last summer," Ruth laughs. "The good thing is that *everybody* looks like they are having a hot flash. Kind of comforting to share the discomfort."

Headache leaves and returns to her couch. She starts to dream about the beauty of old women. About the beauty of lines and wrinkles and bodies of all shapes and sizes. She knows all things are possible and that dreaming is powerful, especially for tricksters. She suddenly sees all kinds of aging women all around the world—not as simply old but as changing and transforming into other kinds of beauty. She sees that all women, including young women, are constantly transforming and that all of it is life. The transformations are about living, loving, learning, experiencing, resisting, fighting and absolutely being—all the richness of living that Val could feel in her grandmothers' skin.

Returning to the tricksters' lounge, Headache studies all the potential trickster power around her. She is thinking, "It looks like we have some work to do." Headache starts to wonder about organizing a trickster seminar on aging. Could be a lot of fun...

VAL NAPOLEON *is of Cree heritage and an adopted Gitksan member. An associate professor with the University of Alberta in the faculties of native studies and law, she has published in areas of indigenous legal traditions, indigenous feminism, oral histories, restorative justice and governance. In 2010 she was awarded the University of Victoria's Governor General's Gold Medal.*

Beauty Redefined

HÉLÈNE ANNE FORTIN

I am a beauty seeker and portrait photographer. I work to capture the essence of people with my camera.

For many women, being photographed is scary business. So I put myself in their shoes and give them lots of time and patience and love. I invite them for tea so that we can chat about who they are and what they feel is important.

I ask them if they think they are beautiful and if they like to be photographed. The majority answer no to both queries. Yet in the next breath they describe how they want me to photograph their child or loved ones, people whom they clearly see as incredibly beautiful.

We women are tough on ourselves. We have lists of things we don't like about our bodies. Beauty is usually something outside or beyond ourselves. Usurped by the glamour industry, it's defined as a six-foot-tall, size-two fourteen-year-old with long blonde hair and big boobs. And yet I sometimes photograph young women who fit that bill, and they hate how they look.

As a sixty-something, slightly chubby five-foot-one-and-three-quarters-inch-tall photographer, I certainly don't measure up. But my own list of dislikes is pretty short, and except for the odd ache after too much exercise, aging doesn't bother me.

I think I became a portrait photographer because I was searching for my own beauty. As easy as it was for me to see the beauty in others, I kept missing it within myself. In my sixth decade, I can finally own it. And I feel privileged to celebrate the lives of (extra)ordinary, beautiful people.

I don't give a damn about their age or size or gender. It's not their outer shell that I see but their goodness, kindness, sacredness and grace—their love affair with their life and loved ones—that illuminate their beauty.

One day, a lovely middle-aged woman commissioned a family portrait. When she came to review the photographs, she proceeded to turn over every single image of herself. She found it painful to see herself. But she cherished the pictures of her loved ones.

In the end, I simply gave her a gift of a large portrait of herself, hoping that someday she would be able to see beyond the surface and grasp what I and her family naturally saw: a kind, helpful, intelligent—and yes, beautiful—woman.

The Greek root for the word "beauty" links to the notion of being called. When beauty touches our radar, it often ignites one or more of our senses, "calling" us to a state of awe, stirring a deep passion within. But we've become disconnected from this meaning.

So the mantra I've embraced and share with the people I photograph—older women included—is this: Just for today, I will redefine beauty and yield to its important call. Just for today, I will see the beauty in myself and others.

....

HÉLÈNE ANNE FORTIN *is one of North America's leading portrait photographers. Dubbed "the next Karsh" by clients, she has received many accolades for her work, including the Commemorative Medal for the 125th Anniversary of the Confederation of Canada, as well as the Grand Prize for* Canadian Geographic *magazine and for* Photo Life International. *Her work hangs internationally. www.portraitsofyourlife.com*

Desiring

My Last Erotic Poem

LORNA CROZIER

Who wants to hear about
two old farts getting it on
in the back seat of a Buick,
in the garden shed among vermiculite,
in the kitchen where we should be drinking
Ovaltine and saying no? Who wants to hear
about 26 years of screwing,
our once-not-unattractive flesh
now loose as unbaked pizza dough
hanging between two hands before it's tossed?

Who wants to hear about two old lovers
slapping together like water hitting mud,
hair where there shouldn't be
and little where there should,
my bunioned foot sliding
up your bony calf, your calloused hands
sinking in the quickslide of my belly,
our faithless bums crepey, collapsed?

We have to wear our glasses to see down there!

When you whisper what you want, I can't hear,
but do it anyway, and somehow get it right. Face it,
some nights we'd rather eat a Häagen-Dazs ice cream bar
or watch a movie starring Nick Nolte who looks worse than us.
Some nights we'd rather stroke the cats.

Who wants to know when we get it going
we're revved up, like the first time—honest—
like the first time, if only we could remember it,
our old bodies doing what you know
bodies do, worn and beautiful and shameless.

LORNA CROZIER *is a Saskatchewan-born poet and revered
mentor. Since publishing her first collection in 1976, she has
authored fourteen books, edited several anthologies, won
the 1992 Governor General's Award, and served as writer-in-
residence at colleges and universities across the country. Her
acclaimed memoir,* Small beneath the Sky, *was released in
2009.*

Cougars and Spaniels

LYN COCKBURN

From an early age, women get used to being labelled. As little girls, we get called tomboys or little ladies; as teens, we get introduced to the word "bitch." Then there's the "how do I tell this obnoxious man to stop hitting on me" scenario. Most of us—upon rebuffing some male prowler (habitat: pubs, parties, workplace, churches)—have been the recipients of the comeback, "You must be a lesbian."

Among the many possible retorts, here are my two favourites:

(a) "Yes, thank God." (Note that this response is not for use only by those of us who are indeed gay, although straights may wish to explain, "I wasn't until one minute ago, but I am now.")

(b) "No, I am a necrophiliac. Die, preferably from something excruciatingly painful, and I'll jump you." (This explanation can be used by straights and lesbians—perhaps with a slight variation: "Yes, but I'm also a necrophiliac...")

The getting-hit-on phenomenon is likely to continue until we age enough to acquire a new label: cougar. Cougars, it seems, are all women over the age of forty who show any sexual interest whatsoever in younger men. Cougars evidently hunt for prey in bars and on the Internet.

It is a term attributed to the website called cougardate.com, which promotes itself thusly: "Cougardate.com: a fun approach to dating where women are Cougars and men are Willing Prey."

However, please note that you don't actually have to leap into bed with the object of your lust to become known as a predator. All you have to do is be forty-two, fifty-two, sixty-two, seventy-two or eighty-two while gazing upon the nicely rounded butt of a passing male. If you make the mistake of remarking, "That dude has got a great butt," you will instantly be labelled a Cougar.

Should you persist in such observations ("I'd like to see him naked"), you'll be branded a Serial Cougar.

And, if you do a Demi Moore and actually conduct a relationship with an Ashton Kutcher who just happens to be sixteen years younger than you are, you are a Cougar for Life. You will have to get used to the fact that whenever your name is mentioned, the age of your husband will immediately follow.

For example: "Demi Moore, forty-nine, and her husband, Ashton Kutcher, thirty-three, who is sixteen years younger, along with her oldest daughter, Rumer, who is only ten years younger than the thirty-three-year-old Kutcher, attended a gala event Tuesday night. Reports that Moore, forty-nine, was wearing support leggings to hide her varicose veins remain unconfirmed."

The term "cougar" has become so prevalent that there's even a TV series titled *Cougar Town* starring Courteney Cox as a recently divorced woman looking for spice in her dating life. I inadvertently saw a preview of this show and, before I could switch channels, observed that Cox, forty-six, looks about thirty-four, and why shouldn't she be eyeing that guy who looks about twenty-four, is what I asked myself. It is a question to which there is no reasonable answer.

Is this where I mention that Catherine Zeta-Jones is a zillion years younger than her husband Michael Douglas, or that George Clooney's current girlfriend is... Oh, never mind.

The point here is not to compound the problem by suggesting a label for *les hommes d'un certain age* who lust after younger women. It is rather to repossess the term "cougar,"—to own it, to embrace it, to remodel it to suit our purpose, to use it for empowerment.

For example, Demi Moore recently announced she wants to be known as a puma, not a cougar. "I'd prefer to be called a puma," she said in an interview with W, adding, "I'm going to get T-shirts that say 'puma power.'" Okay. So pumas and cougars are synonymous, along with mountain lions, but puma sounds so much more elegant. Did you know that pumas have extra-large hind legs (see reference above to Demi Moore's varicose veins) and can leap up to forty feet across the ground, a handy feat when stalking their prey? Also, pumas evidently prefer forested areas and jungles from B.C. to South America, a fact that keeps them out of bars. Note that people in B.C. tend to refer to pubs, rather than bars, although some of us consider all such establishments to indeed be jungles.

I have a friend in Calgary who says she'd rather be known as a bear. She points out that before hibernation, bears are supposed to eat themselves stupid, an ode to Häagen-Dazs. Then there's the fact that mama bears give birth while sleeping—to babies the size of walnuts who are cute, cuddly and partially grown by the time mama wakes up.

The clincher is that boy bears expect girl bears to have hairy legs and sport excess body fat and to wake up growling.

Any boy bear stupid enough to remark on this reality gets swatted good.

But much as I can see the strength in Demi's puma label and my friend's bear brand, I want to be called a spaniel.

This nomenclature is in honour of my mother, who, like a lot of mothers, was wont to tell stories, some of them true, about her offspring, of whom I was the only one. To various boyfriends. Of mine.

One of her favourite stories included both the family cocker spaniel and me. The spaniel, a darling female of reddish hue, became a member of our household when she was a mere eight weeks old. She cried at night, and Mom would get up to comfort her. "She didn't cry as much as Lyn did as a baby," Mom would say to The Current Boyfriend (we were usually the same age because I was too young to be a cougar—or a spaniel), who by this time had a look of panic in his eyes.

"Had to pin the puppy's ears on top of her head with a clothes peg," said my mother. "Otherwise, her ears would get in her food. Hard to clean."

Mother would pause for dramatic effect while I avoided looking at The Current Boyfriend.

"Same thing with Lyn," Mom said. "She was a very sloppy little girl always getting her food all over herself."

Sometimes if TCB and I had already been out to dinner at a nice restaurant, he would mutter, "Still does."

"I always intended to pin Lyn's red hair up on top of her head with a clothes peg too, but I never quite got around to it," was one of Mother's endings to this story.

If TCB said, "Good idea," we were done.

Women of every age must choose their own occupations, ice cream, lifestyle, cars, beliefs, partners, hobbies (and that includes assessing the male butt regardless of its age) and values. Above all, we must choose our own labels.

I choose spaniel.

LYN COCKBURN *thinks she writes pretty good. A former high school librarian and (obviously) English teacher, she took up journalism as her second career. She currently writes a weekly editorial page column that she describes as erudite for the* Edmonton Sun. *She also composes a column she insists is witty for Canadian feminist magazine* Herizons.

The Pleasures
of an Older Man

HARRIETT LEMER

I remember the exact day it happened—the very
moment I became invisible.

I was strolling down the main street of a funky
Vancouver neighbourhood, enjoying the welcome warmth of
the sunshine and the aroma-rich coffee-house ambience. I
felt fabulous.

In front of me walked a beautiful young woman. I was
twenty paces behind and could see her sway past a group of
young men seated around a table, all pumped up, laughing,
talking and posturing.

I watched them watch her. Their heads turned in unison,
an unvoiced collective approval of the lovely woman who had
improved their afternoon. She kept her gaze straight ahead,
her only acknowledgement of the attention a little extra wig-
gle of her hips.

The ritual was familiar, and my anticipation unconscious.
Confident, I sauntered past. But the coffee drinkers remained
unstirred. No following look, no confirming smile, no flattering wink.

I was stunned: barely forty-five, I had suddenly become
transparent.

I stumbled through my errands on automatic pilot and drifted home to my darling husband, Ron, in search of an explanation.

"When," I pleaded, "did my beauty fade to black?"

He listened. He thought. And then he gave me the gift of his thirteen additional years of wisdom:

"You just need to walk into a room of older men," he said. "Your beauty is intact, but your point of comparison is off-kilter."

One of the many pleasures of being married to an older man is the context he gives me. I don't feel diminished by growing older.

I view the new spots and lines on my face and body as testimony to my vintage-wine qualities. I see myself as Ron does: forever beautiful.

Proud of my age-given grace, I now glide easily past young men and into the arms of my own generation.

....

HARRIETT LEMER *lives and works with her husband, Ron Einblau. Together they have a twenty-five-year-old management consulting business, a thirty-two-year-old daughter, and three ten-year-old dogs. She does not spend her time getting face lifts, body wraps or Botox shots.*

Skin and Bones

MAXINE MATILPI

From a distance, I look pretty good. I'm five-foot-ten and a healthy 143 pounds. I faithfully attend my Wednesday-night ballet class and follow the advice of my teachers, always remembering to wear an imaginary diamond brooch at the centre of my chest—which means I have excellent posture. I live on a Gulf Island, and sometimes as I walk in the forest, I notice my own grace, my balanced and smooth deer-like gait.

My husband finds my deerness sexy, tells me that sometimes when he's skinning a deer, he thinks of me, naked.

And sometimes when we're in bed, he strokes my back, and as his hands glide over my bones, he tells me he thinks of that doe, hanging upside down and naked in our shed, its skin peeled off its lithe body, its flesh exposed and ready. Vulnerable.

He touches my thighs and says he can feel sinew, tells me his favourite cut is the loins, that he likes the fineness of my bones.

Fifty-six herring seasons here on the West Coast and I'm settling in to this body.

This is what fifty-six looks like. *Warning: Never use a magnifying mirror except to deal with your eyebrows. The rest you don't want to know.* I think Nora Ephron may have said this, but lots of women have had similar thoughts. I'm thankful my husband's eyes are as bad as mine and I take care not to come within eighteen inches of him if he's wearing his reading glasses. He doesn't need to see the details any more than I do.

When he skins a deer, he sees everything, gets intimate with that deer. He spreads its legs open and goes in where the sun don't shine. Twenty-five years ago, when I was pregnant— *ripe*—with our first child, he massaged my perineum with vitamin E, in there where the sun don't shine.

Another time, when our three boys were young, one of them—or maybe all five of us—got some kind of intestinal worm, and my husband had to make a return visit with some special diagnostic tape to check for eggs from the worms, to see if the bright-pink medicine had done its job. These are the benefits of mature love, the comfort of familiarity.

Now our boys are fully fledged men, making us empty nesters. We sit at the kitchen table by the window of our Gulf Island home, just the two of us, slurping hot deer soup, the broth sticking to our lips. We lick the bones and suck the marrow, and he tells me *again* that he likes how I look. This is the luxury of growing old together, the time and distance from intestinal worms, the memories of fawns and placentas, the blurring of each other's wrinkles.

....

MAXINE MATILPI *is Kwakwaka'wakw and lives and works on Vancouver Island in Coast and Straits Salish Territory. She works at the University of Victoria law faculty, where her research interests are indigenous law and indigenous pedagogy. She spends weekends on Denman Island with her husband, gardening, swimming, walking and thinking about riding her bike.*

Advocating

The Shady Side of Fifty

CONSTANCE BACKHOUSE
....

I stopped dead in my tracks the first time I walked past the Famous Five monument on Parliament Hill. Passers-by rarely glance at the other statues that grace the landscape of our national capital, but most strollers who cross paths with this one stop and smile. An inspirational example of public art, often described as the most popular in Ottawa, the monument offers a gloriously festive spectacle. Captivated by the tea-party setting, I sat down in the empty chair that seems specially designed to entice people to share the elation of the Five: Emily Murphy (author and Alberta police magistrate, the first woman to preside over a women's court), Louise McKinney (the first woman elected to the Alberta legislature), Irene Parlby (also elected to the Alberta legislature and who, when appointed minister without portfolio, assigned herself special responsibility for women's rights), Nellie McClung (acclaimed author and feminist activist), and Henrietta Muir Edwards (for many years the Convenor of Laws for the National Council of Women and Canada's pre-eminent feminist legal expert).

The celebratory tea party is in honour of the legal victory in the Persons Case, decided in 1929, which finally opened the door for women to sit in the Canadian Senate.

As I lingered, savouring the quintessentially female feeling evoked by the five larger-than-life women's statues, I watched scores of others stop, sit down and take their photographs. Many stayed to read the description of the Persons Case and to marvel over the bad-old-days when inequality seemed so visibly entrenched across our political process and legal system. Some also mused about the women who had had the temerity to challenge the gender exclusion, and others commented on their old-fashioned dresses and hats, which must surely have been *au courant* in the time but which looked so quaint and out-of-date today.

Much has been said and written about the lives of these remarkable five feminists. That they were visionaries of indomitable imagination and spirit is beyond debate. That their understandings of equality did not always encompass issues of race, ethnicity, class, sexual identity and disability has also been the subject of critique from feminists and anti-feminists alike. As yet, however, few commentators have focused on their *age*. This oversight surely means that the discussion misses one of the central features of the case. Quite likely, I would have missed this in the past too. Now, at the age of fifty-eight, with a mother who is eighty-eight, I find my antenna becoming more attuned to age.

The Famous Five were not young women when they conceived of, campaigned for and then joyously celebrated the victory of the Persons Case. Nellie McClung, the youngest, was fifty-five. Irene Parlby and Louise McKinney were sixty. Emily Murphy turned sixty the day the case was argued. And Henrietta Muir Edwards turned eighty the year the case was won.

Their role in the Persons Case poses an interesting study in contrasts. The "Roaring Twenties" was not an auspicious era for older women or feminists. The women memorialized during that age were young "flappers," who smoked, short-ened their skirts, bobbed their hair and pursued sex in the rumble seats of motor cars.

Pundits sneered at feminism and wagered that wom-en's causes had already been won. The suffrage had been extended—to some; the first female MP, Agnes Macphail, had been elected. Critics maligned the aging female reform-ers, asking what more they could possibly demand. They insisted that the new generation of women had little time for feminism. Yet in these times that were distinctly unfriendly to feminism, it was *older women* who had the courage and fore-sight to bring the Persons Case to court.

As a long-time researcher and compulsive reader of wom-en's history, I have been struck by how often I have been inspired by feminists from the past. During our twenties, thir-ties and forties, "second-wave" feminists of my generation frequently drew sustenance from the ideas, strategies and life stories of "first-wavers."

Today, for many second-wavers who have gloried in the activism and adventures of the women's movement over the past five decades, the topic of age has become increasingly rel-evant. Many of us have now passed the midpoint of our lives, some have begun to retire, and all are taking stock of what the feminist movement has achieved, what we have failed to change and what uncharted vistas await. As we pass through our fifties, sixties and seventies, will we fade from public view, or will we regroup, recharge our energies and forge ahead on wonderful new projects to dismantle misogyny and change the world? For aging second-wavers, the older women who have gone before have become even more inspirational.

In addition to the Famous Five, I celebrate the remarkable Elizabeth Cady Stanton, a nineteenth-century feminist who led the American women's rights movement for almost fifty years. Stanton urged older women never to think that their "life work was done" and wrote that "the hey-day of woman's life" was "the shady side of fifty." Her biographer described her as "a defiant old lady." In her sixties and seventies, Stanton contended with physical ailments, retirement, financial insecurity, the death of friends, family estrangement and generational conflict. But she "survived her husband," "outlived most of her enemies" and "exhausted her allies."

Glorying in both her venerable age and her undiminished radicalism, she titled her autobiography *Eighty Years and More*. Challenged by blindness and obesity in her later years, she joked that although her legs and eyes were "weak," "my voice seems to hold its own." At the age of eighty, she published *The Woman's Bible*, attacking the use of scripture to condemn women to secondary status. The opus was characterized as "her most audacious and outrageous act." Newspapers heralded her as "the Grand Old Woman of America." Her biographer concluded: "Her mind remained alert, her mood optimistic, and her manner combative." Stanton's final years were characterized by "undiminished militance."

An American feminist who is more our contemporary, Gloria Steinem, founded *Ms.* magazine in 1972, a publication often described as the second-wave's most influential periodical. A marvellous activist, Steinem took her campaign for equality from "brown-bag lunchtime lectures organized by office workers" to "housewives' self-help groups" to "all-night rap sessions at campus women's centres."

Her travels brought her to the conclusion that "women may be the one group that grows more radical with age." She noted that older women have the luxury of having navigated beyond the uncertainties of trying to find a career and a mate, beyond having children and discovering who is responsible for them and who is not, and past the insecurities of youth.

She explained that older women have built up vast experience with discriminatory educational systems, workplaces, families, politicians and cultures. She argued that such expertise was essential to a "feminist revolution" that would "rarely resemble a masculine-style one." Steinem challenged us to uproot the sexual caste system that lay at the heart of the most pervasive power structure in society. She forecast that "one day, an army of gray-haired women may quietly take over the earth."

Mary Daly, another American second-wave contemporary, also celebrated older women. A radical feminist philosopher and lesbian separatist, whose death in January 2010 sparked an outpouring of feminist tributes, Daly wrote groundbreaking texts that reclaimed formerly derogatory words such as "hag" and "crone." In her book *Gyn/Ecology: The Metaethics of Radical Feminism*, she explained the origins of the terms, arguing that traditional definitions, because they were written by misogynists threatened by women's power, actually rendered the words complimentary.

"A Crone," she wrote, "is one who should be an example of strength, courage and wisdom," and she proudly took for herself the title of "Profoundly Revolting Crone."

As a young feminist, I began work in the fields of violence against women and workplace discrimination—areas where the devastating destruction wrought by sexism was in high relief. The enormity of the damage emphasized the urgency of the task. Gradual, slow-paced change never appealed to me. Nor did gentle campaigns for reform, designed to soft-pedal discussions about injustice and harm. I was drawn to feminists who took pride in radical ideas and transformative strategies. It got me into a lot of trouble, but I tried to say what I really thought and to aim high when asking for change.

The prospect that I and other feminists, who were publicly and privately chastised for demanding too much, might become *even more radical with age* is something that has always made me smile. Our movement has left a lot of work still undone. We need an army of white-haired, wild-eyed radicals cutting a swath against the sexism that crosses our paths.

It is a good antidote to the larger community's apparent belief that older women are slightly dotty, grandmotherly, benign souls. Now on the shady side of fifty, I find it distinctly off-putting that so many service people feel comfortable addressing me as "dear" or "dearie"—even occasionally patting me on the head as if I were slightly less than human. Do they not know that feminists become more dangerous with age? Perhaps we need a button that reads: "Beware! Aged Radical Feminist."

Inspired by our historical fellow travellers, I hope that our generation of feminists will embrace aging, revelling in a passage of life that can offer new opportunities for rebellion and transformation. I would urge us to endeavour to outdistance the Famous Five in their glorious upset of the legal assumptions of male superiority and female exclusion. I will dream of fundamental cultural revisioning of the scope of Elizabeth Cady Stanton's *The Woman's Bible*. I think we should all adopt Mary Daly's titles of *hags, crones, harpies* and *furies*. I want us to participate in the march of "gray-haired women" on the "shady side of fifty" and in the "hey-day of their lives."

In these days, more than ever, I believe we need the wisdom of aged women. Our revolutionary capacities are endless.

....

CONSTANCE BACKHOUSE *holds the positions of Distinguished University Professor and University Research Chair at the Faculty of Law, University of Ottawa. A legal scholar who uses a narrative style of writing, she is internationally known for her feminist research and publications on sex discrimination and the legal history of gender and race in Canada.*

From Feisty to Respectable

ELIZABETH MAY
....

It may be difficult for some to say "so long" to the
occasional wolf whistle and skin that bounces back,
but aging has great appeal for the activist woman.
I used to be seen as a disruptive influence. Rebellious. Feisty.
Now I'm respectable. It's a welcome change.

As a young female activist, I occasionally faced derision.
Sexism and ageism combine to make young women the butt
of jokes. As a twenty-three-year-old waitress on the Cabot
Trail, I used my tips to finance a campaign to stop aerial
insecticide spraying on the forests of Cape Breton Island. For
my efforts, I was compared to a French sex symbol.

"The seals have Brigitte Bardot and the budworms have
Miss May," declared the *Chronicle-Herald*.

Budworms are not quite the telegenic species that seals
are, and larvae are nothing compared with big-eyed pups. Of
course, my campaign was not to protect cute little budworms;
it was to stop the widespread distribution of a toxic chemical.
Our main concern was human health. But the media's attack-
by-analogy would never have been made against the medical
doctors and researchers working on the issue. The ridicule
factor only worked because I was a young woman.

Moving from waitress to lawyer helped my credibility. But
the young woman lawyer faces some of the same contempt,

as American activist Bella Abzug discovered the hard way. (That's why she wore her famous hats: she was tired of being mistaken for a secretary. "Secretaries do not wear hats," her husband told her.)

Age doesn't end all misogyny, but once I cruised past forty, well, the level and tenor of abuse toned down a bit. And, although I still get nasty barbs from some unfriendly quarters (like the blog postings of angry men who ask when I will go on Jenny Craig), being an elder in the movement—and an Officer of the Order of Canada—gives me some peace.

Mostly the calm centre comes from being over fifty. For me, this means that children are grown and that achieving life goals represents less a race up a mountain and more a navigation of well-worn paths. Experience brings some wisdom. This is a great time to be a woman. No longer am I hoping everyone will like me. No longer do I care.

I think of women I have admired who shook the world in their fifties. Bella Abzug. Gro Harlem Brundtland. Ursula Franklin. And my contemporaries and friends—Maude Barlow, Vandana Shiva, Wangari Maathai, Margaret Atwood.

Whether women speak from a background of science, policy and law, medicine, or the arts, we bring something else, too. Whether we are actual mothers or not, our voices are heard as a voice for children, for future generations. It is not for nothing that our planet is so often called "Mother Earth" or "Mother Nature."

And as we ripen into our forties and fifties, distractions decline. We have no time for fussing about diets and hair; every day requires getting useful work done. We can be fearless. Uncompromising. We can embrace the word "feminist"!

Being a strong and capable woman in her fifties is a good place to be. It calls on one to mentor younger activists. That network of women—young, old and in the middle—maintains the continuity of celebrating the female energy in the world. As I look forward to the short hop across the years to sixty, I am able to breathe easy, claim my space and feel good in my own skin—even if that skin is sagging, streaked with stretch marks and bears a really impressive hip replacement scar.

Fifties are the best decade—so far!

....

ELIZABETH MAY *is an environmentalist, writer, activist, lawyer and leader of the Green Party of Canada. She has authored seven books, including her most recent,* Losing Confidence: Power, Politics and the Crisis in Canadian Democracy. *Elizabeth became an Officer of the Order of Canada in 2005.*

Finding My Voice

SHARON CARSTAIRS

A voice is a powerful thing—when you learn to use it. We are all born with the ability to communicate. As babies, we cry. As toddlers, we start to speak. Part of growing into adulthood is finding our voice—learning how to communicate effectively with those around us.

As a young child of nine, I was sexually abused by a family friend. I could not find my voice to speak out to make the abuse stop. I was afraid my abuser was right and that I would not be believed if I told. I was terrified of how my parents would react if I told them their friend had betrayed them. I felt isolated, as I thought I could not tell my friends, my parish priest (who was also a friend to the abuser) or my teachers (who were nuns and, in my view, to be protected from this). And yes, I was silenced by my shame that this was happening to me and by my inability to stop it.

It was several years later—when my younger sister caught the eye of my abuser—that I found my voice and spoke out. I told the abuser that if he did not stop, I would tell. The abuse stopped. Unable to find my voice to protect myself, I found it to protect my sister. That act of speaking out was a pivotal moment in my life. I learned that I need not be silenced by my fears. I learned that by using my voice, I had the power to seek change.

As a young woman, I became a senior high school teacher. My deep, gravelly voice could silence a gym full of rowdy tenth graders with ease. Projecting my voice so as to be heard by fifteen- and sixteen-year-olds was always a simple matter. And yet what was such an asset in the classroom became somewhat of a liability when I entered politics.

When I started in public life in the mid-1980s as a provincial politician in Manitoba, the media and the public were much too preoccupied with my clothes, glasses, hairstyle and, most particularly, the sound of my voice, to bother engaging me in public debate. My voice had a peculiar quality to it that—magnified by television and radio recordings—sounded much higher pitched when broadcast than in person. I received almost as many letters commenting on my voice as those commenting on my politics. In the early days, my critics were too busy listening to *how* I was saying something to listen to *what* I was saying.

But as a politician, I haven't allowed this to stop me. I've used this quality in my voice to continue to gain attention for the issues I'm passionate about. I do believe that being a woman has been an advantage to me in my public life. I take a different approach to politics and to public policy than most men I have worked with. I have been most interested in the issues that have the greatest impact on society's most vulnerable. And I have striven to represent those whose voices have been silenced.

In 1987, I was the first to oppose the Meech Lake Accord, although I was soon joined by others. In 1990 and in 1992, I again spoke up, along with others, against both the Meech Lake and Charlottetown accords.

Since being appointed to the Senate in 1994, when I was in my fifties, I've been a passionate advocate for health care and criminal justice reform and for research and education into abuse and neglect, in all their manifestations. I have used my voice to advocate for human rights, for an end to violence against women and children and for better care for seniors and the dying. I've spoken on behalf of those who are vulnerable, whose voices go unheard.

Having now passed my sixty-fifth birthday, a curious thing has happened. That mysterious quality in my voice, which served me well in the classroom but which was said to sound strident in the electronic media, seems to have changed. Or has it? People approach me and ask if I have taken voice lessons or speech therapy. I've had neither.

A voice is a very personal thing and not easy to alter. Has the physical quality of my voice naturally evolved with age? Have the media and the public just grown used to female voices talking about public policy? Or have they just grown accustomed to *my* voice? In any case, people no longer comment on my voice but instead engage me in debates about public policy.

But this has not been the only change. With the life and work experience I've gathered behind me, I have the confidence to use my voice as never before to advocate for those denied their own. I feel great about my voice—and about using it!

....

SHARON CARSTAIRS *became the first woman to lead the Official Opposition in a Canadian legislative assembly (Manitoba) in 1988. Appointed to the Senate in 1994, where she continues to serve, she is the author of* Not One of the Boys, *the co-author of* Dancing Backwards: A Social History of Women in Canadian Politics *and a contributor to* Dropped Threads.

Struggling to
Become an Elder

JUDY REBICK

"Hello, My name is J'Moi Whyte. I am in grade ten and attend R.H. King Academy in Scarborough. For my history assignment, I was assigned Judy Rebick. Hopefully this is you."

I'm a history assignment now?

My initial reaction to the email I received over the Christmas holidays was horror. The pleasure took a little longer.

Aging in a youth-obsessed society is a complicated matter. I was never much of a beauty, and men were always more interested in my mind than my body, so that part of aging has had little impact on me. When I was in my early fifties and famed feminist writer and journalist Doris Anderson was in her seventies, she explained why she loved aging.

"Older women are invisible," she explained. "I can look at as many young men's asses as much as I want and no one even notices." A round of hearty laughter followed, but I was a little surprised at this from Doris, whom I'd thought of as rather a prim and proper older woman. Of course, we had never talked about sexuality before that.

But now I am approaching sixty-five, and although I have more energy than most, I am noticing signs of aging in both body and mind. Unlike Doris, I am not satisfied with just looking, and to my total astonishment, I find that an amazing number of young men want nothing more than to have an affair with an older woman. Maybe we can thank Helen Mirren or Meryl Streep for showing the world that you can be female, sixty and still sexy; maybe these young men grew up with strong women; or maybe the interest was always there and it's just easier to find with the mainstreaming of online dating sites these days. Unfortunately, the feminist principles that led to disapproval of older men seeking younger women has caused me to restrict my own sexual practices, after an initial enjoyable tryout.

As a heterosexual who did not find a lasting partner when I was young, it is tough to find an available man my age with whom I want to spend a lot of time. As a result, I find myself mostly in intimate friendships with younger men, the benefits of which are legion but not sexual.

Politically, I've become more radical as I age: questioning the politics I spent my life defending—not to promote something more conservative but to question the whole rotten system.

And in what might be a parody of aging, I have become interested in spirituality for the first time. Not because I am thinking about dying but because I have found that some people who are into spirituality seem better able to have the kind of relationships I admire—loving, co-operative, honest and challenging.

Really, in the last few years, I have changed more personally and politically than in any other time of my life. I don't know if it has to do with aging or with a feeling that my political activism and that of most people around me has been hitting a brick wall, but I have been able to shed some of my old assumptions and open my mind and heart to new ways of seeing the world.

When I started work on my most recent book, which documents many of these changes in thinking, I found it difficult to get going. This was very unusual for me. I usually decide I want to do something and then just do it. In the parlance of the day, I am very entrepreneurial. In the early 2000s, I started a number of projects—like rabble.ca and the New Politics Initiative—as a way of responding to my concern about the decline of the left. Even when they succeeded, they didn't seem to be making as much of a difference as I had hoped. I had a strong feeling that powerful new forces for change were emerging around the world, but their formation was not yet clear. In an interview, I told a Latin American activist that I wanted to capture what I saw. He responded, "No, you can't capture it—only describe it. It is in a constant state of flux." I thought my fear was about writing a book that had more questions than answers.

But when I examined what was stopping me in an exercise during a powerful U.S. leadership training program I attended in early 2006, I realized that the real fear was about changing my role. Instead of leading something new that would transform things, I would be using my privileged position in the university and my political wisdom to find out what was already happening in various places around the world and sharing that knowledge in the hope that others would run with it. I was giving up the role of leader and embracing a different role, more similar to a traditional elder.

The concept of an elder is something I've learned from my Aboriginal friends. When I was president of the National Action Committee on the Status of Women (NAC) in the early 1990s, I noticed that Sandra Delaronde, the Aboriginal vice-president, always consulted with the elders in her community before making a big decision. For example, when we were discussing what NAC should do in the referendum on the

Charlottetown Accord, where all of the political parties, governments and even our allies in the labour movement were supporting a Yes vote, she brought a shawl that her elders had given to her to represent the wisdom of the ancestors. Even though at the time I was quite skeptical of spirituality, I could feel the wisdom of those elders in the room helping us to come up with a very difficult and controversial decision. They didn't tell us what to decide, but they did help us to take the risk of saying No.

But in European culture, there is little respect for elders. Moreover, most of us don't act the role of elder, still taking up too much of the space of leadership instead of supporting and advising young people. For me, it is a struggle to move into this role, not because young people don't want to listen to what I have to say but because it is so hard for me to drop the identity that served me so well most of my life.

After facing my fear, I wrote the book. I started in Latin America, where I knew there were important forces, not the least of which were the indigenous movements—especially in Mexico and Bolivia—that were reinventing progressive politics. But in my research, I also found young people in the United States and Europe doing some very similar things. So instead of thinking of the book as an intervention into the politics of the day, I wrote it as an observation of the new politics that I saw emerging. The book was so outside the political discourse of the mainstream media that they virtually ignored it. Young activists and students love the book, and it's selling well, but it didn't get the attention I was used to getting for my books, and that bummed me out. An elder doesn't get the attention of a leader, and I am still working on being okay with that.

When I tell women close to my age that I want to move more into the role of elder, they often express sympathy for me, as if I am giving up and retreating. But that's not how I see it at all. I think there is a rhythm to life, and it makes sense to ride with it rather than fight it. I've rarely done what's expected of me, so conformity isn't what I'm talking about. Instead, what I know is that I have a lot of knowledge and wisdom to share, but I don't have the energy and stamina that's needed to lead a struggle, mount the barricades or battle it out day by day. And I don't want to do it anymore. I've spent a lot of my life in confrontations. I can still stand down a bully or a blowhard, but it's not how I want to spend my time or energy.

Sometimes when I am speaking, an older man will ask why young people don't seem to want to hear from their elders when we have so much to teach them. I usually answer that if he could drop his critical approach and listen first, he might find they were quite interested. What I hear young people saying is that they want support, inspiration and wisdom from their elders.

Sharing stories is powerful, too. I remember my surprise at how little young women knew about the extraordinary women's movement in Canada when I released my book on the subject. In an interview about feminism recently, a journalist told me she was amazed by how unfamiliar the young women she had interviewed were with feminism. Their mothers were likely involved in some way or another in the magnificent struggles that profoundly changed women's lives in their lifetimes, and yet they know little of what it took to get to where we are. That's not their fault; it's ours.

The role of Aboriginal elders is to keep the history of their people alive through their stories. Even though I am part of the dominant settler culture in Canada, I hold many stories of the battle against patriarchy on both a personal and a political level that I want to share. I see the calm and grace of Aboriginal elders, and that's what I would like to achieve. Maybe it's a little against my nature, but I'm going to keep trying.

I notice that friends my age who retire face a serious crisis. It seems to me that we're among the first generation of women who defined themselves primarily through their work. In my case, it was political work, rather than a particular career. For my mother's generation of full-time wives and mothers, aging was different. It was the menopause, and seeing their children go off to university, that often provoked a crisis. For me and my peers, the identity crisis is more likely to hit—as it does for men—at the age when we're expected to start thinking about retirement.

Those of us in or near the baby boomer demographic fight aging with all our energy. "Sixty is the new forty." What a load of crap that is. Instead of fighting the inevitable— whether with plastic surgery or by refusing to make space for the young—we should see the later stages of life as a time to explore new possibilities. Surprisingly enough, I think that aging gracefully is really what can keep you young.

....

JUDY REBICK *is a social justice activist, writer, educator and speaker. Her latest book is* Transforming Power: From the Personal to the Political. *Currently holding a chair in social justice at Ryerson University, Judy has also worked as a journalist and as publisher of rabble.ca. A lifelong activist, she is best known for her work in the feminist movement.*

Celebrating

Dinner Tastes
Better than Ever

ALISON SMITH

Nearly every winter, our family travels to the Eastern Townships in Quebec to stay with friends
at their family farm.

We've been doing this for nearly two decades now. It's a
ski trip when the snow is plentiful. But no matter the weather,
it has become a shared tradition among three families—the
stuff of wonderful memories for our children.

When we first started, the trips were a jumble of puffy
snowsuits and runny noses. A continuous counting of heads
to keep track of the growing "ski team" of small children
spread among the three families. A day on the slopes meant
countless visits to the bathroom, endless buckling and
unbuckling of boots, and constant reassurance that, yes, we
would go inside soon for hot chocolate.

For us, as young parents, it was a happy, exhausting mara-
thon. Oh, how we looked forward to the end of the day. That
was our time—our holiday time.

With our children in bed or ensconced in front of a movie,
we gathered around the dinner table in the farmhouse. Cooking and eating together have always been a big part of our
friendship. We were a group who met in our twenties and ate
together throughout university. We celebrated graduations,
first jobs, first houses and kids.

So, at the farm, planning the food, preparing it and, of course, eating it always seemed like a celebration of friendship. Fresh oysters. Seared duck breast. Long-simmered turkey soup. Lobster dripping with butter.

By candlelight, our faces glowing from a day outside, we savoured the tastes and talked and laughed long into the evening. It was as if we didn't want the meal to end. When we'd finally rise from the table, we would crank up the music and dance while we did the dishes.

Our children, for so many years, were observers to the rituals and pleasures of those meals. Often, they turned up their noses at the too-fancy food. As teenagers, they sometimes listened to our conversations about politics or education, but usually they scurried to the basement to play Ping-Pong, scornful of our blasting Motown rhythms and embarrassed by our dancing.

I still smile when I think of those evenings.

Now, my children and their "farm friends" are the same age I was when we all met. At the ski hill, we're in and out of the lodge in an instant. Our strapping sons easily shoulder the family pile of skis and poles and boots.

They wait patiently on the slopes while we nurse our creaking knees around the moguls.

Still, there's great pleasure as we all gather in the early evening in the kitchen and at the dinner table. But now it comes seeing my twenty-two-year-old son slurp those oysters just as eagerly as his dad. Or from watching his older brother carefully lay out appetizers—pork rillettes and pickles he made himself.

The dinner table is once again ringed with glowing young adults. Over a steaming plate of paella this year, I often found myself just watching and listening. Childhood giggling has turned into teasing banter among good friends. Young curiosity and energy enliven our conversations about such things as the war in Afghanistan or the health-care debate in the U.S.

My friends and I exchange those proud, smiling glances that parents share in moments when you know your children are happy.

The years have made the pleasures of the table richer. For me, dinner tastes better than ever.

....

ALISON SMITH *is a senior correspondent for* CBC News *and the host of* CBC Radio's The World at Six. *Over more than three decades, she has reported from Europe, the Middle East, South Africa, South America and every province and territory. Most recently, Smith was a Washington correspondent covering the historic election of Barack Obama.*

Facing the Void

DAWN RAE DOWNTON

....

PISS OUTSIDE: so said the scrawled sign tacked to the wall of the airport waiting room at Sachs Harbour, a tiny settlement (pop.: 100, more or less) on Banks Island in the Arctic Ocean, where temperatures can fall to minus fifty degrees. Evidently, the building's proprietors had not contemplated that a woman might need to fly in or out of Sachs Harbour and might need to pee if she did.

So said the sign in the early seventies, at least, when my husband hitched a ride there on a single-engine Otter making its way down to Yellowknife from the DEW Line. Is it still there? Place your bets. Whereas peeing prefers women, especially as they age, peeing policy prefers men. Consider another sign, the one posted on the roads and in the parks and town squares of Germany. A stick-man arcs away inside a circle sliced diagonally by a line: it's the familiar symbol for *don't,* and the sign means NO PUBLIC PEEING. As if a woman could stand and arc like that anyway, in public or anywhere else. In Germany, voiding how-tos are strictly the purview of men.

Same in Cambodia, where signs dictating toilet etiquette show side-by-side views of a stick-man peeing. On the left, he's X'ed out where he's squatting unaccountably *on* a flush toilet, his feet lodged on either side of the bowl. (Honest. You can't make this stuff up.) On the right, he's sitting on the throne instead. No X through that. Whatever other questions this raises, why is he not using a stick-urinal? Don't they have urinals in Cambodia?

Maybe they don't. Whatever the rules of the john the world over, there's that whole tricky business of international latrine design. Sitting toilets dominate the West (plus Cambodia, evidently), but in most of the developing world, you squat—where you can find a toilet at all. Even Dubai lacks enough wcs for its commoners and labourers, who find themselves in the holding position of women worldwide.

But Western travellers, beware as well. Those gleaming tiled stalls with grateless floor drains at the Dubai airport— the ones that look like showers? They aren't.

Worse, sometimes you can't contort yourself into position and have to lean back on your hands. Worse still: "The first thing I realized," reports a man in off a flight from Perth, "was that dropping my pants did not give enough 'clearance.' I would have to commit and take them right off. It then occurred to me why Arabs wear skirts, and it all made perfect sense."

Here's a real plus of aging—in the West, at least: privy progress. These days you usually pee for free. (Remember when you didn't?) These days we have taps that know, toilets that talk and antibacterial self-flushers in Sears Bargain Basements. In Norway, where *haute* heads take credit cards, the entire room scrubs itself after you leave. All this, and no squatting anywhere.

ONCE UPON A time, bathrooms were for holding up the family, for squeezing blackheads and perfecting your hair. Back then, the only emergency was my sister's—she always wanted to get in. And so I ignored my mother's grim warning, whenever we climbed into our Vauxhall Viva for a road trip, to "go *now*; we won't be stopping." Back then it was me and the mirror, nothing more.

But then I went to Athens. I went with my high school, as part of a two-week tour of the Mediterranean that was meant, I think, to "broaden" us. We flew into Gatwick and then down to Venice—where it had just snowed for the first time in, like, ever. Snow in Venice, for God's sake. What a piss-off. It was all we thought about: you see what you know. The Bridge of Sighs? Can't remember it. I don't remember finding a public loo, either, or worrying that I wouldn't. I was fourteen. It wasn't an issue. I do remember that my sister was flashed on the outskirts of the old city. We were young enough, and this was back in the day enough, that we had no idea what in the world this guy was doing. And wasn't he cold in the snow?

From Venice, we boarded a stripped-down Norwegian cruise liner that needed retiring. Don't remember a thing about the heads. There must have been heads, though everyone used the passageways to be seasick. I do remember leaning over the deck rail to stare at the water coursing far below. Men will tell you that all that coursing gives them the urge, but instead it made me fear that my glasses would fall off and be lost to the deep. God. What would I do then?

We day-tripped to various ports: Athens, Valetta in Malta (incredibly, Valetta had a Bank of Nova Scotia; don't know about latrines—at fourteen, I had an armoured bladder), then Casablanca, Lisbon and, finally, Southampton. Wow. The *Titanic* had sailed from Southampton. A few people—perhaps a dozen women among them—were "booked to sail" but didn't. Mrs. Charlton T. Lewis. Miss Wilkinson. Emma Duyvejonck. Were they in their fifties? Were they charmed? Did they miss the boat for being in the can? There must have been cans in Southampton, but back then, I didn't notice.

They'd've been for a whole other set of women: those *Titanic* women, the kind of woman, at fourteen, I knew I'd never be— with the kind of bladder I knew I'd never have.

As for Casablanca, when we disembarked there, I recall that the blondes among us had to memorize an international phone number to call in the event we were kidnapped by nomads. (Can this be right? Am I making it up? Where would we have found a pay phone? Would it have taken Canadian dimes?) I recall, too, with depressing clarity, how I boarded the ship again at the end of the day. I was blonde and I'd been stared at, but I hadn't been carried off.

But I can't tell you about *les pissoirs*. Since it was Morocco, that's probably just as well.

In Athens, though, the toilets were plenty memorable— even though I never saw them. We stayed late in town, and when eventually we did find things coming to a head, we ran to a public square and found the sign to the latrines. But at the bottom of the stairs, none of us could find the light switch for the women's side. Urgently, we groped the walls, inside and out. No way we were going into the men's side—not after that guy in Venice. But the switch simply wasn't to be found, and its absence became part of the mystery of using the facilities themselves.

We inched our way in. There they were, just as we'd been warned: unspeakable holes yawning in the floor, footrests on each side—apparently. We couldn't see, after all. Still, I'm not making this up—trust me. I remember how the valiant among us poked around, then squatted wide—really wide— and how the cowards held it.

I held it. I sure remember that.

IT'S AN OLD story for women, holding it. Men, in contrast, can pee anywhere, anytime, in any weather—and they do. They write their names in snow. They have arcing contests over car hoods. Wharf piss-offs are *de rigueur*; bridges, too. (Two guys are walking on a bridge. "Let's pee over the side," says the first, and they do. "Sure is cold," says the first. "And deep," says the other.) Another contest, in the tradition of tomcats, is the marking of oceans. With the Pacific, the Atlantic *and* the Arctic oceans all under his belt, my husband's a comer there. But mostly men go against walls—as Mick Jagger, Keith Richards and Bill Wyman did, famously, in 1965 at a U.K. petrol station when the pump boy, unsure what he was dealing with, withheld the key to the facilities. They were fined £5 each.

Men can even pee against a bus full of nuns, and I'm not making that up either.

My first husband did it. He was a man of marvels—a musician in a military band that travelled around representing the Queen. Road trips were party time, and those in the band who liked them, liked them a lot.

When the band bus made a pit stop one day, squeezing in alongside the nuns' bus where it was parked beyond the pumps, he staggered down the steps and lurched into what seemed a convenient, discreet corridor between the two. Why bother asking for the men's room key? Why bother lining up? He unzipped in front of a tire more than half his height (like dogs, men go for tires), the nuns looked down and crossed themselves, and he found himself returned to base forthwith, enrolled in DOD's famous "coffee course." There he was shown a week's worth of car crash pictures and told not to drink again, at least not so much, and please, not on the job anymore.

Those in the band who liked the coffee course liked it a lot, too; it was a paid week off work. Its lessons, whatever they were, generally failed to stick, and recidivism got you at least another paid week off. Ex himself graduated from two coffee courses and then fell off the bandstand, with his tuba, during ceremonies at the Canadian embassy in Washington.

He liked to make a splash. Did I mention the time he stopped in front of a bathroom display at Home Depot?

SHIT HAPPENS. Things change. Once I was fourteen with that armoured bladder. But when I got to university, I began to disarm. I was arcing towards something after all, but I didn't know what, or why. Might it have been all the Keith's, or the all-nighter coffees before term paper deadlines and mid-terms and finals?

For a dentist, I used the university dental clinic. Most students did. Attached to the dental school, it was a teaching clinic, and it was cheap. There was a waiting list. When you finally got in, there was also a personal health questionnaire. I don't remember what was on it. The usual family history, I suppose. Whether you might be pregnant, or presently suicidal, and so on. But here's a question I do remember: *Do you urinate more than six times a day?*

Duh. Didn't everyone? I ticked the Yes box.

The thing was, by the time we got to university, we all peed more than six times a day, me and my girlfriends—lots more. We didn't know why the dental clinic cared, but we couldn't imagine who didn't pee that much and more, or why not. We had pee to spare. We made up pee jokes. "Don't piss me off," we'd say about a prof, the prime minister, the head of Air Canada (same service then as now). "Don't piss me off or I'll pull down my pants and pee on your lawn."

We didn't realize then that one of us would really do it. That I would. On Anne Murray's lawn.

Anne hails from Springhill, two hours north of Halifax. In the early seventies, she left for Nashville, L.A. and Glen Campbell, and then she seldom came home. Well, fine. After she's seen Paris, how're you gonna keep her down on the docks? When eventually she bought oceanfront near Peggy's Cove, we were surprised. We weren't surprised that she did it quietly. But we had a friend nearby, a spy, and we knew.

Anne's land had a nice fringe of forest along the back and, at the front doorstep, a glorious view of the ruined wharves of St. Margaret's Bay, its jewelled sunsets, its gulls wheeling overhead. We waited for Anne to build on it, turn up in the summers, swing on her verandah humming "You Won't See Me," maybe even lunch at the Cork and Pickle up the road.

She didn't. She never came. The land lay vacant, ignored, stood up. It didn't seem right. Tony Americans do that to Nova Scotia. They buy up our waterfront, spiking property assessments and pushing out the locals who can't keep pace. Then they show up, maybe, for a week of yacht racing in July. Now here was Anne, once one of us, doing it to us, too— hoarding a vacant stretch of resplendent Maritime coastline. Anne's gulls wheeled over nothing; Anne's sunset unseen.

One August weekend, moths to the flame, we meandered through Anne's fringe of firs on the back of Anne's abandoned lot. We'd been into the inevitable two-four of Keith's at our friend's place nearby. What can I say? We were so easily amused back then, and Anne had pissed me off. It felt like freedom. It felt right—a relief. Perhaps it felt as it had for Mick and Keith and Bill Wyman. It felt as though I *had* the right, for once. "Nobody owns th earth," the poet bill bissett wrote, and, having to study him in Canlit 217, we laughed about that too. Of course somebody owned th earth. Men did. They peed on it.

MEN HAVE ALWAYS had the freedom of the stream; women, never. At fourteen, it didn't matter to me. But lately, I'm developing that talent, the men's talent, for peeing anywhere, any time, and not necessarily in a toilet. It's not convenient; it's not something I asked for or wanted; it means I could get stared at, though not in the way I was stared at in Casablanca. I was young then; now I'm not. But hey, it's an arc.

Doctors inform us that many of the drugs seniors take have anticholinergic properties and side effects; that is, they dry you up. If you're not a senior—if, like me, you're merely an intermediate—get yourself on those drugs anyway. Be prepared.

Or else set your sights on living a little, as men always have. Go to Sachs Harbour. Go anywhere. Piss outside.

DAWN RAE DOWNTON *wrote the memoirs* Seldom *and* Diamond: A Memoir of 100 Days, *and* The Little Book of Curses and Maledictions for Everyday Use. *She freelances for magazines and newspapers like* Maclean's, *the* Globe and Mail, *and the* National Post. *A Newfoundlander, she now lives with her husband on Nova Scotia's south shore.*

At This Stage: More Wholly a Fool in Bright Orange Boots

A play with words

SHEREE FITCH

Empty Stage.
Inuit throat singing begins as Me enters. Me is a fifty-something woman with hair the colour of a dirty penny. She is barefoot and wears a thick terry-cloth housecoat. A huge duffel bag is slung over her left shoulder. Me stops centre stage, puts bag down, rubs her shoulder. Rotates the socket, wincing slightly. Throat singing gets louder. Me looks skywards as she listens in wonder. Volume increases. Lights flash above Me and shine on her face, giving the effect of aurora borealis until the throat singing ends, as it always does, in laughter. Lights above her stop flashing. Me steps in a puddle of light and squints as she looks out into the audience. If there is one. It doesn't really matter—or does it?

Me begins speaking as she raises her arms and opens her palms in a kind of joyful surrender or what could be understood as a hallelujah or maybe just oh shit what's next could you give me a freakin' break. Then Me shrugs and breaks—into a grin.

ME: This stage isn't just another stage... *this* stage this just past middle age stage is a coming of age stage out of the cage stage a sage age the allowing myself to rage stage stargaze stage a strange stage the crone age find myself alone [a lot] stage

quite possibly… deranged stage a most certainly
    rearranged stage
here now! hear now!
is *this* the now or never stage
?
guesswhatitis… is what it is

This is the stage on which you get to:
    sing to bling to do your thing
    to dance to prance advance from motherhood to
        (M)otherhood to

OTHERHOOD: find another neighbourhood do the world a bit
    of good
    take more chance find romance

*[Me hops, opens legs jumping-jack style. Looks between her
legs, back to audience, back to vagina and yells encouragement
to her vagina.]*

ME: wakie wakie daylight in the swa-aaamp!
    tromp on tromp on rock 'n' roll 'n' really live!
    forgive, give up whatever shame stage end any kind of
        blame game
    forget who's got a name game lose that ego fame game
    no need for armoured games just open up your arms age
        charm age
    for ME IS much more FREE… [pause]
    free to——
    to zip to soar to let it rip to sip more wine to zoom to find
    more rooms… of Me's own… [pause]
    rooms to write some poems from
    bigger rooms to roam from
    even go to Rome—Come!

even grow some home grown ... pot ...
a-toes potatoes pot of toes
rutabagas green tomatas
o yes ... scribblegabblebabble
go fast go slow but let let let let go keep letting go
now's the time to chime in rhyme to shout! to let it out
    to blow
that lid [I think Me did] to pout to rant to cut the can'ts
    to rave to chant

Ommmmmmm. woooooooommmmmmmannnn. ommmm.

[Me presses hands to heart in prayer as she omms for a bit.
Omms stop, and she strikes a boxing stance and dances around
as she continues.]

ME: It's the: forever I will engage stage the varicose veins in my
    legs stage eat my eggs in my bed stage baggy eyes but wise
    age learn to love my thigh size a witchy bitch mixed stage
    gonna raise more hell stage sort of set in my ways stage
    praise whatever God stage
    Ahhhhhhh!
    to pray today this way stage
    to play stage hey ho stage
    ever ready for sex stage [you only only wish stage]
    steady steady stay stage turning the next page stage
    lift the words off the page stage.

Or not.

ME *breathes deeply. Stills herself. Plunks down cross-legged.*

ME: Look. It's the now i really know i don't know stage except the know i now know i don't know is a better know than the know i never knew before stage you know or maybe you know you don't know too stage

but…still it's all the world's your stage age [Me stands back up; does a 360-degree turn.]

ME: finally get to Greece stage naked on a beach eh? take a trip to Nice hey…

[Me clears her throat and takes a bright turquoise beret from her pocket and puts it on her head.]

ME: Excusez moi? oui oui maybe you and me some café in paris
café au lait today stage
yes! yes!
buy myself a *grown-up* dress…

[With this, Me throws off the terry-cloth robe. She is wearing a stunning black evening gown]

ME: TADA!

ME *does an exaggerated imitation of a supermodel on a runway. Sucks in belly, lifts up breasts, stuffs beret in her bosom, takes it out, puts hat back on head, walks, swiggle sways from side to side, posing and pursing lips. Bows. Blows kisses. Then stops.*

ME: Upstaged offstage increasingly no wage stage don't need to wage a

major war stage bones creak like squeaky doors stage body
     kinda
sore stage rusted inside out age K-Y Jelly Depends stage
     not quite
bad as that yet—speaking for myself stage!

shuck the fears stage
drink your beer stage

but... *[angry] fuckin'* lot of tears stage
so much pain stage tears like acid rain age
heart split wide apart days

friends are dying waaaay too often waaay too young stage
[pause]

ME *[hushed voice]*: unavoidable truth: I. *can't. help. or. heal.
the. ones. I. love. the. most. truth*

that puts me
in
a
sad
rage
death cage knock knock hard knocks
heart ache heart quakes hard knocks
death breathing down our necks cage

so pass the die stage past the die stage cast the dye stage
     the dye is past so kiss the joy as it flies stage... because
     it does eh?...
no longer can you lie stage...
stop trying so goddam hard stage...
but keep whying flying high stage!

[Me flies, flailing arms like wings, makes zooming sounds as she flies and flies until she is out of breath, stomps her feet to full stop. Me is Motionless for thirty seconds.]

ME: AHHHHHHHHHOOOOHHHHHHHHHHAHHHHHH! *[or whatever primal whoop explodes]*

[Me throws up her head like she is ready to do a Zulu warrior dance. She is. African drums begin, and Me does some weird kind of spastic ecstatic dancing for a bit. Drums fade. Me's exhausted and plunks down on the stage but is laughing in exhilaration.]

ME: Okay. So. What's left in this old bag? I mean that one, not me.

[She points to the duffel bag. Hops towards it. Begins to open it when a doorbell rings.]

OFF-STAGE VOICES: Delivery for Me!

[Me walks cautiously to stage left.]

ME: But I never ordered . . . but . . .

OFF-STAGE VOICES: Special delivery-for Me. Call it an unexpected gift. There will be
more. Not all of them quite so comfortable.

[Two women enter, carrying a sofa. Me signs for the delivery. Me examines it. Tests the pillows. Sits down. Sighs contentedly. She moves; the sofa moves. She moves it back and forth, like a kid with a toy.]

ME: Hey it's a … a … stage couch …! Get it? *[an offstage groaning.]* ouch.

ME *[defensive]:* hey it's the i can make bad puns stage have a
lot of fun stage idjit critics didn't your mother ever tell you
if you can't say something nice just shut the F#$% up …
excuse my language and it's not my hormones. It's the I'm
less needy to be liked stage less greedy to be needed stage
and everyone's connected euphoria
o gloria Epiphany!
Everybody's ONE hey, overwhelming love stage …
ommmmmm
no door mat but no baseball bat no victim but no victor
over other either
everybody vulnerable
I digress. The bag. What's in the bag? *[She snorts in glee.]*
Kind of like my version of wilderness tips. Wildness
tips. I said tips not tits. Survival gear.

*[Me reaches in the bag, and as she speaks, she brings forth
these items.]*

One pen.
two pens red pens blue pens
any many many pens
a book what book
The Cloud of Unknowing by Author Unknown
lipstick Tampax *[She throws this over her shoulder.]*
a photo album

*[Me hugs this to her. Rocks back and forth a bit then opens
the album slowly. She keeps turning pages, her face a revolving
door of emotions as a sound collage begins, baby being born,
sirens, weeping, children squealing, planes, hymns, the Bee*

Gees singing "Staying Alive," voices, slamming doors, gradua-
tion music, waves, birds, a mix of life sounds of joy and sorrow
until she shuts the book and stares blankly into the audience.

A baby cries. She runs across the stage looking for source...
laughter of child... fades... Me rubs her belly. Walks slowly
over to couch. Curls up.

Silence for several seconds. Inuit throat singing begins softly.
She sits up and reaches for bag once again. She pulls out a pur-
ple shawl and wraps it around her. Then out come her bright
orange boots. She laces them up. Finally lime green gloves that
go up to her elbows.]

ME: This stage is the:

    time to be outrageous stage let joy be contagious stage you
        must be courageous stage...

    and sometimes just just shut up and listen stage *[She does.]*

[Throat singing a bit louder...]

ME: rage against the dying light stage

    dance on fearless into darkness...

    look at me a holy fool in this get up... this get up and go
    keep going on

    to... the next stage... *[She holds hand out to audience.]*

ME: come sing and be merry and join with me and sing the
    sweet chorus of ha, ha, he
    if you dare

[Me leaves, making a lot of noise in her boots.]

[Empty stage.]

[Aurora borealis strobe-light effect searches the audience. Throat singing ends. In laughter.]

SHEREE FITCH *is a poet, a speaker and the author of over twenty-five books in a variety of genres. Since the 1987 publication of* Toes in My Nose, *she's travelled the globe as storyteller, literacy educator and writing teacher. Her adult novel* Kiss the Joy as It Flies *was shortlisted for the 2009 Stephen Leacock Memorial Medal for Humour.*

Bump-Her Stick-Her

ANN ST JAMES

B ump-Her Stick-Her is a game that specifically targets women over the age of fifty-five. Research indicates that women in this age range appreciate a good stick as much as boys under the age of seven. And like young boys, older women prefer bumps to hugs. There are no winners or losers in this game: the model is co-operative, not competitive. The game is simple: a stick is passed from one hand to another only after one bum exuberantly engages another.

Step one: find a stick. When you are out walking, pick up a few sticks. Any shape and any length will work. Artistic types will turn this step into an adventure: fascinating sticks will end up on display in the den. Craftswomen will transform their sticks into dolls or totems. Any tendency with a stick that brings you joy should not be inhibited. But for most women, like most young boys, beauty is not a requirement. Any dirty old wrinkled up stick will do. The gnarled sticks may even prove to be the most treasured. A word of caution: later in the game, you'll be giving the stick away, so don't become too attached.

Step two: spot a Her. The Her must be over fifty-five, and the Her is not eligible if she is recovering from hip surgery.

Your local grocery store is a good location. Wait for Her to be stationary. For example, Her may be choosing a can from a shelf. Move near Her. Position your back to Her back, then let your bum hit hers. Bum-to-bum contact. The harder, the better, but not so hard you knock Her off balance. This is a deliberate action on your part—nothing accidental about this manoeuvre. Her will expect you to say sorry. So you will surprise Her when you say, "So glad that I bumped into you." You then turn and offer your own bum. As you turn, you say, "It's your turn to bump me back." After Her bumps you, move to the next step.

Step three: reach into your purse and pull out your stick. Put stick in Her's hand and say, "Stick Her." Bear in mind that there is no deep or hidden message here. A stick is a stick.

A final note: trust yourself. As you may have discovered in other aspects of life, your unique style of playing will give you more joy than the recommended version. Do not rigidly adhere to instructions. Flexibility and fluidity fuel fun. Relax and let your Her enjoy the bump and the stick.

ANN ST JAMES *has been writing plays for thirty years. As well, she administered a Waldorf school and supervised a residential unit for emotionally charged adolescents. Tap dancing is her current joy. Twice a week, Ann and a gaggle of old gals giggle with delight as they tap-tap-tap.*

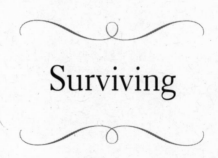

Surviving

Living beyond Loss

SUSANNAH COHEN DALFEN

On a gloomy May day, Chuck, my husband of forty-two years, clutched his head and was gone. All that remained of the man I so deeply loved was his unyielding body. Chuck, still wearing the suit that had been slashed by paramedics in their efforts to revive him, could utter no word of goodbye. I was forced to say mine, standing horrified, with my shocked and stricken daughters, in a cold hospital emergency room.

Together, Chuck and I had raised these two marvellous young women, walked them down the aisle to loving men, thrilled to the birth of their children and found ways to be proud grandparents to four astounding children. We had grown up from our early teenage fumblings, emotional and otherwise, to embrace our more mature years. As a couple, we took much joy in our daily walks and stretching sessions by the river or on hikes amidst the subtle nature of the Gatineau Hills. Our travels took us on a wide range of excursions to Machu Picchu, on safari, to India and Nepal. Further plans to travel, study and live in other parts of the world were hatched on our morning walks.

Challenges that life threw in our path, including a bout with cancer and a life-threatening accident—both of which

Chuck had sustained—we confronted as a team. We became more appreciative of our differences. On occasion, I was stunned to find that we had achieved greater depths and joy in our relationship.

Together, we celebrated meaningful Jewish rituals. Each of us brought our own skills: I, cooking, and Chuck, a beautiful, melodic voice and depth of knowledge and understanding. Earlier in our marriage, on such occasions, I had hoped, mostly in vain, for some sharing of the culinary duties. But over the years, even I mellowed, and my expectations faded.

Our life included close relations with family and friends— it could get no better for me. I could not conceive that all this shared existence could be gone in the time it took some errant plaque to block an artery.

As my being absorbed the shock of suddenly losing Chuck, I was struck by the understanding that the long, warm, embracing friendship and love that we had nurtured and grown between us—especially in the last decade—was no more. I was alone to carry on in the world. Left with memories dating back to my teenage years of us together, I am now a single woman in a society structured around couple life. I am now labelled a widow.

The very term made me bridle with indignation. It was as if I were being cast in a different mode. Adding to the already enormous loss of my life companion was a loss of societal status. I hadn't changed myself into another creature, as the word seemed to suggest. Yes, I was living in absence and loss, but to be labelled a widow meant to me that I was now considered to be living in relation to the past—in relation to a husband who was gone. A fully lived present and future were to be beyond my own hopes for myself.

The term "widow" dates back to Old English and was first cited in AD 825. It originates from the Latin word *vide*, and apparently came from the word *widh*, meaning to separate, to be empty. It was used in a phrase with the word "orphans." In combination, the two words connoted a group of people who lived in loss and outside the mainstream of social interaction—a group to be pitied and possibly reviled.

So when, on occasion, I have been called "the widow," I have snapped back, "I am not a widow!"

I am a single woman living with visceral memories and loss—bereft of my husband and the warmth and protection that my marriage provided. Now I live alone with no choice but to make my own way in the world, trying to figure out what it means to function without a partner: to awaken in a quiet, still bed, half of which lies undisturbed; to return home to a silent house from which no welcome emanates.

But I am trying to refuse to present myself as a person whose existence is no longer to be taken as seriously, as one who lives on in absence and is now less important.

Aging is difficult enough; the marginality that comes with it in our society seeps in surreptitiously. With the exceptions of medications and retirement plans, advertising focuses on youth. Fashions are geared to the young with firm skin. The thumping music in restaurants is played to attract the youthful ear, repelling the more sedate and hard of hearing. A multitude of conscious decisions need to be made daily to affirm one's relevance.

My husband, who had filled senior government positions, even as a young man, was seen by many colleagues, friends, family, children and grandchildren as a true presence—full of life, engaged and delightful. At times, I sailed in his enormous wake. He was vital—a force of nature. I also recognized that some of the status he had achieved by virtue of his accomplishments and talents adhered to me and enriched my life.

Several clubs, which Chuck had been invited to join years ago and which we had always attended as a couple, notified me of a change in my membership status. I regarded this as unacceptable and have since fought—successfully—to have myself reinstated.

The good fortune life has bestowed upon me can no longer be taken for granted or as something that I somehow deserved. I am now forced to remake myself, to delve into my own resources, to rely more on my own counsel, to manage the mundane demands of everyday life—to take out my own garbage and to process my own thoughts.

Now I am faced with making my life an expression solely of myself. The relationships I seek out, the activities I engage in, the way I decorate my home—are all of my own making. In some ways, I am confronting independence for the first time in my life, having been twenty when I married. My newly acquired BlackBerry connects me to my friends and family. It's a companion in bed and on the road—a bit of technology that helps to distract me from my loss. I look for new relationships with both women and men and find that my connections to many people with whom I already had a closeness have intensified.

Travel, which I had always loved with Chuck, and which had initially been a source of our recognized compatibility, is now a different experience. When travelling with friends and family, I face an empty hotel room—a stark reminder of my aloneness. But I am entirely free to decide when and where I go. Recently, I invited my seven-year-old granddaughter to join me on a trip to New York City—a bonding, fun-filled adventure, enabling me to see the city through a child's awakening to the larger world.

My own world I carry with me wherever I go. I am no longer a sequestered part of a larger whole; "we" has become "I."

At times, I struggle to assert myself, to push against my internal walls, to be more engaged. Having been forced to abandon the naïve sense of certainty with which I had thought of my future, I wonder what life will bring me.

Truly, I am bereft in the absence of my dear departed partner, but I am also alive in and to the present, both its challenges and its promises. My current path forces me to embrace my own life.

SUSANNAH COHEN DALFEN *was born and raised in post–World War II Montreal. She studied economics and art history at McGill University, married young and followed her husband's career moves across the country. While raising their two daughters, she earned a master's in social work and is currently a practising therapist and volunteer with a range of community organizations.*

My Colonoscopy

GAIL KERBEL

Thank goodness for our internal organs—without them my girlfriends and I might have run out of conversation years ago. It seems that whenever we get together, no matter where we begin, we end up discussing the intimate details of what's happening inside. From first period to first orgasm, from pregnancy to childbirth and on to menopause, our histories are told in tales of plumbing.

The menopause conversation entertained us for almost a decade, but now that our hormones have regrouped and settled down, there's not much left to say, and we have moved on—to our colons. Just a few weeks ago, five friends were over for dinner, and before you could say, "Is it warm in here, or is it me?" we were talking about our recent colonoscopies. It was fabulous! Let me tell you, if you haven't yet reached the age (fifty), when the doctor says it's time for your first routine colonoscopy, you have something to look forward to.

Over farfalle with roasted squash and arugula salad, each of us shared the story of her bowel prep, and though the narrative was pretty much the same, it was important that every woman have her moment. There were a few variations: Brenda's purgative was banana flavoured, a detail that brought forth richly nauseated moans, but Joan's choice to go without anaesthetic was most impressive. We yelped and grunted as she described the colonoscope navigating the sharp turn around her uterus. And then we had dessert.

For me, the best part of the colonoscopy was the hollow sensation that followed slugging back twelve gallons of evacuant. It left me feeling purified—almost holy. It was in this divine state that I floated into the clinic on the morning of my procedure and met my gastroenterologist. Something about the man was vaguely familiar, but I wasn't sure if I knew him or if he reminded me of Jerry Lewis. I stood there in my socks and open-ended hospital gown, squinting at him, trying to figure this out, when he glanced at my chart, looked up and said, "Hi Gail—remember me?"

"Huh?"

"It's Lubo... Lubo Kransky?"

Right, Lubo Kransky. We went to high school together. Lubo was one of those nerds who stood in the hall with his pals and giggled as girls in tight sweaters walked by. Back then, I hung with a pretty cool crowd, and Lubo Kransky barely entered my consciousness. I guess you could say that I was "in," and he was "out." But in the cold white examining room at Lubo's clinic, the table had turned, and I lay upon it, exposed. While the anaesthetist set up his equipment and the nurse took my blood pressure, Lubo and I did what you do on these occasions: we played Jewish geography.

"So, how's your cousin?" he wanted to know. "Still playing viola?"

"Um, I don't think so, but she's fine, thanks."

"Good. How about Shelley Whatshername, Shelley Weinblatt? You still see her?"

"Shelley Fineblatt. Yeah, sometimes."

"God, she was beautiful. Is she still?"

This was neither the time nor place to be thinking about how beautiful Shelley Fineblatt was, and I might have said so, but the sedative took hold. I was out, and Lubo was in.

Shelley was one of my best friends in high school and was famous for her loveliness; you couldn't refer to her without someone saying, "God, she's gorgeous," or something along those lines. She was a striking mix of cute and exotic, and this incongruence held your gaze as you tried to make sense of her face.

Everything about Shelley was beautiful: her laugh, her gait, her handwriting. All through the early grades, I wanted to be her friend, to catch some of her light, and finally in high school we became pals. Together we ran that mad dash through the teen years, from the end of childhood to the brink of adulthood. We shared the intimate details of our relationships with boyfriends, comparing notes as we progressed from first base to all-the-way; we analyzed the flaws of our other friends, prepared for a life of artistic brilliance and cracked each other up. I adored her.

And yet, as our friendship deepened, a feeling crept in that took little bites from the satisfaction of our closeness. I became envious of the very qualities that attracted me to Shelley in the first place. I began to resent the advantages her beauty granted. Teachers loved her, and every boy I had a crush on wanted to go out with her. I drew feeble pleasure when a zit sprouted in the dainty fold of her nostril or when her hair went frizzy. Most of all, I wished that I could live in her skin and know what it was like to be exquisite.

Forty minutes after my chat with Dr. Lubo Kransky, I emerged from the anaesthetic, ravenous and rather gassy. Lubo was in a chair beside me with my chart. His earlier question about Shelley had been knocking at the edges of my anaesthetized mind, and now I was struggling to respond, but, groggy from the drugs, it came out something like, "Howzit beautiful now."

"Well, I was going to tell you it looks fine," he said, "but okay, your colon looks beautiful. See you in five years."

My husband was in the clinic lounge waiting for me. On the car ride home, I wolfed down the tuna sandwich he'd brought and thought about my relationship with Shelley. I remembered that feeling of envy and how it twisted my gut, how it was more painful than menstrual cramps. I thought about how I'd struggled to hold my conflicted feelings inside, to prevent my bitterness from leaking out, and how exhausting that was. I looked forward to the day when we would all be as old as our mothers (thirty-nine) and wouldn't care about what we looked like anymore. And then it occurred to me that I'm older than my mother now, and I do care. When I was lying in Lubo's examining room suffering from caffeine withdrawal, loopy from hunger, and wearing nothing but a bluish hospital gown, I was waiting for him to say, "Gail, it's been a long time. You look great!" But he didn't; he asked about Shelley.

Of course, in the grand scheme of things, given a choice, I would rather hear that my colon looked great, but we are rarely in a situation where we have to choose between our colon and our face, so there's little comfort there.

No. Great comfort is found in knowing that all my friends passed their colonoscopies with flying colours. I didn't feel the slightest twinge of envy. How wonderful to know that everyone's gastrointestinal tracts looked beautiful. Of course, we'll never actually get to witness this, unless someone buys a colonoscope, but that's unlikely. One of the great things about getting older is we don't have to see beauty to know it's there.

....

GAIL KERBEL *is an actress and writer living in Toronto. She has written animation, sitcoms and documentaries for* TV *and contributed many hours of comedy to* CBC *Radio, including twenty* Stand-up Documentary *specials with her partner, Chas Lawther. In 2007, they were nominated for a Canadian Comedy Award for their television show* Is It Art?

Of Birthdays and Bibliotherapy

ANN COWAN

Over a decade ago, when I turned fifty (which had just become the new forty—or was it thirty? About the same time a size twelve became a size ten—or was it eight?), I announced to my gathered family and friends that this would be the decade of death. It came to me in a champagne-induced flash that one or both of my parents might die, and God forbid, possibly my husband, who was of my parents' generation. What a way to spoil a party!

Fortunately, talk turned to the forthcoming celebratory trip to Italy, recklessly financed by cashing in an RRSP, but the idea that my next challenge was to learn how to live with death had lodged in my subconscious. Of course, it was learning how to live with *other* people's dying that concerned me then; consideration of my own mortality would wait a decade.

In the intervening years since that fiftieth birthday party, both of my parents and my husband *have* died, and an uncommon cancer of the neck has forced me to plan my own endgame. The endgame in chess is played when there are just a few pieces left on the board; it is also the name of a play by Samuel Beckett, which I studied along with William Wordsworth's "Intimations of Mortality" as an undergraduate.

Bibliotherapy and retail therapy are my usual supports when faced with any life crisis—the former reminding me that whatever is happening to me has happened or been imagined before, the latter providing a distraction. I've already bought a condo, and my bank account is pouring down the drain of its expensive bathroom sinks—appropriately called vanities—and so the time for bibliotherapy is at hand. No longer living in a house of many books, I googled Beckett and Wordsworth to good effect. One of the great dividends of aging is the ability to fully appreciate words that were wasted on me in my youth:

> Though nothing can bring back the hour
> Of splendour in the grass, of glory in the flower;
>   We will grieve not, rather find
>   Strength in what remains behind;
>   In the primal sympathy
>   Which having been must ever be;
>   In the soothing thoughts that spring
>   Out of human suffering;
>   In the faith that looks through death,
> In years that bring the philosophic mind...
> Another race hath been, and other palms are won.
> Thanks to the human heart by which we live,
> Thanks to its tenderness, its joys, and fears,
> To me the meanest flower that blows can give
> Thoughts that too often lie too deep for tears.
> WILLIAM WORDSWORTH, "Intimations of Mortality,"
> 1803–06

The Wikipedia page that conjured up Wordsworth in a keystroke was sponsored by an advertiser wanting to reveal the "One-Minute Trick of a Tiny Belly." Being a curious person, I clicked on the ad, and there was Rob, the same disaffected formerly fat autoworker from Michigan who had tried to sell me the TRUTH on a former Amazon/Google excursion and who sorrowfully asked me what he had done wrong when I closed his window mid-pitch. Full of Wordsworth's reminder that we live by the tender human heart, I connected with the primal sympathy and decided Rob and his ex-fat wife, Kalen, deserved another chance. Rob was offering a Push-Button Fat-Loss scheme, which would ignite my Fat-Burning Furnace and turn my body into a Fat-Burning Fitness Machine (a new definition for hot!). I could have the FBF plan for $39.97, the ULTIMATE FBF for $69.97—or if I bought it RIGHT NOW, for $39.97, the same amount as the economy version! And, what is more, I could download it and have INSTANT GRATIFICATION.

Never before had bibliotherapy and retail therapy morphed so seamlessly. But I had indulged in RT just yesterday, and, cozy in my silver sage cashmere robe purchased on sale from Restoration Hardware, where the restoration seems to lie in selling lifestyle vanities, not nails, I closed Rob's window once again, despite his renewed apology for offending me and his plea to accept a FREE Fat-Burning Fitness trial.

It did occur to me that dying is also a fat-burning strategy. As the Tibetan Buddhists describe it, the elements leave our bodies in the order of earth, water, fire and air. In my observation, this is indeed true—hence my reluctance, facing the endgame, to push that Fat-Burning Button just yet.

The characters in Beckett's *Endgame* and *Waiting for Godot* are both sad and funny, having arrived at a "philosophic mind" that turns not to Wordsworth's "Fountains, Meadows, Hills and Groves" but to trash cans, cold park benches and the hopelessness and subtle irony of it all. They are a sorry lot, as Mother would have observed, and it occurs to me that we die more or less as we have lived, horrible accidents and untimely death notwithstanding. I vow to stick with Wordsworth's blowing flowers and concentrate on thoughts "too deep for tears."

So what is the task of aging? Popular media suggests we do our best to preserve the appearance of defying the grim reaper. I have a drawer full of anti-aging potions for various parts of my body and am always pleased to be told I don't look sixty-two; and although I don't dress like my daughter, I don't dress like my grandmother did at my age either. But there is no escaping the fact that in twenty-five years, should I live that long, my hands will have the same ropey veins as Mother's when she died last month. She did not love her hands, but I loved her. I wonder if my mind, as hers did, will become tattered at the edges. Will working at crossword puzzles and Sudoku and practising bridge and yoga or the hot sex recommended by *Zoomer* magazine help? Or what about positive thinking? Is that the answer? My daughter, Juliana, has suggested more than once that negative thoughts manifest themselves—causing death and cancer. I doubt I have such power one way or the other.

Orson Welles observed that "We're born alone, we live alone, we die alone. Only through our love and friendship can we create the illusion for the moment that we are not alone." We may be happier and more self-confident and have more friends in old age if we remain attractive physically, and many studies support the notion that society prefers the thin and good looking. We even know that attractive patients get more attention in hospital, so Rob and Kalen might be on to something. Nonetheless, I sense that aging requires a better endgame than physical attractiveness, friends and love, because I have seen beauty shining forth when the mind and body have failed.

When my sixtieth birthday arrived, I had no grand tour planned, no inclination to make pronouncements on the next decade—my greatest desire was to spend it with my mother, without whom, as they say at the Oscars, I would not be here today.

My mother's home in Petrolia, Ontario, is an attractive and spacious apartment at treetop level, offering a bird's-eye view of the house where I spent my early childhood and the street where I rode my bicycle through the dying embers of bonfires on cool October evenings, sending thrilling showers of sparks into the early-falling darkness. The dining room windows are filled by the rose window of the Presbyterian church next door, an oddly comforting intimacy not available at street level.

Mother's life that year had a rhythm that is easy to adopt, a combination of meals and walks and naps, closed each day by watching the sunset. The strategic spot where she placed her chair takes in the whole panorama of the western sky. Many things had left her life—the ability to travel to exotic places, to manage her own affairs (although she remembered that she sold Nortel at $120), to read a book every day, to swim twenty lengths of the pool morning, noon and night—but she has this marvellous sky that never disappoints her. She tracks the phases of the moon, even though the day of the week, the month or the year might elude her.

In her mind were constellations of memory: that weekend she focused on the day of my birth, remembering how even though it was the first day of classes, my school-teacher father insisted on staying home, how he waited all day in the hospital waiting room and how excited he was. I tell her that she was the age of my daughter when I was born and that I am now the age of my grandmother at my birth; but she is not interested in these calculations. What do they have to do with the happy memory and excitement of that new life all those years ago?

Back in Petrolia, where Mother and I confronted the essentials, which that evening were birth, death and closing the windows, much that occupied my life seemed unimportant. I realized that I could write a page or more on Leonard Cohen's wonderful line, "There is a crack, a crack in everything; that's how the light gets in." Especially on the delicious repetition of "crack" and the comma, which provides the crack in the phrase to let the sentence breathe and meaning to creep in like light. Does he mean the crack in my heart left by my husband Peter's death, or perhaps the crack in the pavement, which would break my mother's back, had I stepped on it all those years ago?

As I walked with Mother that afternoon, the ironies of cracked sidewalks surfaced. Mother was charting a familiar course with her walker—she knows the smooth and bumpy streets and walks accordingly. The cracks have rearranged themselves in the fifty years since my sister and I strapped on our roller skates, tightened them with the key that hung from a ribbon around our necks and skated forth in search of smooth pavement. Mother and I tried to remember who had lived in which houses, remarked on well-kept gardens, who had been seen lately out-of-doors, who was ill, whose children came to help. And then home to make dinner, listen to music and watch the sunset.

How much is enough to make life worth living? How do we face the truth that we are alone, regardless of who is by our side, at the end of our last breath, at least during that passage from the material world? I've come to think that the best way to "lighten up" is to give some time and thought to these questions. At this stage of my life, such thinking feels somewhat like planning for a trip, and it seems important to leave behind emotional baggage that can weigh one down. Googling "the unexamined life is not worth living" to make sure I had Socrates straight, I was directed to a short essay by Karl W. Palachuk, who urged me to subscribe to his free newsletter, "Relax, Focus, Succeed: A Newsletter for a Successful Life." Karl also supplied a reading list, which, oddly, had no poetry on it.

P.B. Shelley was right—poets and philosophers are the "unacknowledged legislators of the world," with the emphasis on unacknowledged! Karl brushed over the fact that Socrates was sentenced to death for encouraging such examination, and I realized that plans for a successful life are a bit short on advice for planning a successful death, relegating such thoughts to "negative thinking," which is not one of the recommended seven habits.

Every spring I like to read T.S. Eliot's *Four Quartets* and "Ash Wednesday." I always find lines I have missed before and believe that as the decades proceed and the meaning deepens, such lines give us a particular liberation.

> And what the dead had no speech for, when living,
> They can tell you, being dead: the communication
> Of the dead is tongued with fire beyond the language of
>   the living...
> History may be servitude,
> History may be freedom. See, now they vanish,
> The faces and places, with the self which, as it could,
>   loved them,
> To become renewed, transfigured, in another pattern.
> T.S. ELIOT, "Little Gidding," 1943

It strikes me in my Lenten mood that addressing the challenges of aging, preserving the mind and body as best we can and holding our nearest and dearest in our hearts are a form of servitude, and our challenge in our last days is to break free of the self and become "renewed, transfigured in another pattern." For now, I'm a happy slave to the life of the mind and the body. I enjoy each day with friends and family. I'll shop till I drop and lose myself in beauty, but my endgame project is to find that state of grace, that other pattern Eliot describes: "What we call the beginning is often the end. / And to make an end is to make a beginning."

....

ANN COWAN *was born in Petrolia, Ontario, where her teachers and family encouraged her love of literature and ambition to study at the University of Toronto and later Carleton University. In 1977, she moved to Vancouver. There, she and Peter Buitenhuis shared poetry, raised their children and worked at Simon Fraser University.*

A Work in Progress

BONNIE SHERR KLEIN

I'm writing this en route to the funeral of my twenty-
year-old great-niece, Miriam Deborah Frankl.
Miriam was struck down before her prime by a
drunk driver near Johns Hopkins University, where she was
entering her third year. She was a budding molecular biolo-
gist who was thriving in the benefits for which we earlier generations of women fought. This is a cruel moment.

I look down at my hands, writing. Fingers gnarly. Every
joint swollen. Lumpy. Turning in unnatural directions. (My
long-fingered hands were once my best feature—piano fingers they were called, though my piano playing didn't match
their grace.) Prominent veins on freckled skin. We used to
call them "beauty marks," but they are now skin damage, age
spots.

Painful, too, aching from the stress of tightly gripping
walkers, scooters, canes, especially the new forearm crutches.
The space between thumb and index finger is stretched.

Nails are brittle, strong vertical ridges that often split. A
few are thickened. Are they my mother's hands?

I remember trying to clip my mother's nails as her fingers
curled under and pierced her tightened palms. Her nails were
too thick for the instrument. I tried in vain to straighten her
clenched fingers—was it for me or for her?

168

She was in a "foster home" with other old women with Alzheimer's disease, finally too violent to stay in our house. I had broken the promise she had extracted from me that we would never "store her in a warehouse."

I can travel this path of comparison, foreboding and guilt, dreading the old age I have witnessed in my mother.

Or I can take a different route. I can choose to thank these tough hands without which I cannot walk. They took over when a stroke ruptured the circuitry from my brain to my legs and feet. These hands learned to support me for a transfer from bed to wheelchair to toilet. Later, they navigated the various mobility aides with which I walk the earth.

In 1987, I had what was labelled a "catastrophic" stroke, caused by a congenital malformation in my brainstem that erupted spontaneously when I was forty-six years old. It seemed like a bitterly abrupt ending to what had been my privileged life as a healthy woman, wife, mother and feminist filmmaker. Suddenly I was "locked-in," unable to speak or breathe on my own, quadriplegic. My universe shrunk. I went through years of intense rehabilitation. I experienced the classic stages of grief and loss, including clinical depression. It was an instant projection into old age, disability and dependency.

I was sustained through it all by the loving care of my husband, Michael, and our teenage children, Seth and Naomi, who needed me to come back; by our various communities of friends; by the financial security of our professional lives; and by the benefits of the Canadian universal health care system. I have met many people who have survived disability and other trauma with less "success" because of social isolation, lack of financial resources and inadequate health care.

I knew the long uphill climb of rehabilitation, originally steep, would be bisected by the inexorable descent of aging, and indeed my progress did plateau. It has been compromised by arthritis, osteoporosis, cataracts and generally diminishing strength and balance. It would be dishonest and foolhardy to deny the inevitable physical truths of aging.

There are many things we cannot control, but we can choose our role models for aging. In the early days of my stroke, my worried nineteen-year-old son, Seth, asked me what I would do now that my filmmaking life was over. I said I might try to be like the Speaking Our Peace women. That was code in our family for a genre of older women activists.

A few years before my stroke, I made *Speaking Our Peace: A Film about Women, Peace, and Power* with co-director Terre Nash. Our film featured Muriel Duckworth, Professor Ursula Franklin, scientist Sister Rosalie Bertell, Mayor Marion Dewar and writer Margaret Laurence. These women were, each in her unique way, contributing to a culture of peace. They had become my heroes and inspiration, my elders. They helped me get through my stroke, literally and figuratively, and I felt that they were waiting for me now. I wanted to be more like them, on the front lines instead of hiding behind the camera. My promise was comforting to Seth then and is only slowly being realized in the twenty-plus years that have passed since.

I met Voice of Women co-founder Muriel Duckworth when she was seventy-three. We invited her to go to the Soviet Union with us for the film. It was the height of the Cold War. She met and cried with Soviet women of her generation who had survived the Second World War. Muriel was an "ordinary" woman, a housewife before the second wave of feminism (and we thought we had invented the movement!). When Muriel identified a problem, she gathered a few like-minded women for tea or quilting, and an instant organization was formed. Her activism was not a frenetic escape from reality but a consistent and spiritual practice. Muriel's long life was seamlessly integrated—caring for the planet was an extension of caring for her large extended family. In the words of Muriel's good friend, Ursula Franklin, "We send our letters to the editor and write our political briefs just like we do our dishes. It's all women's work." Speaking Our Peace women are concerned not about the material but the real legacy we pass on to our children.

Muriel became my surrogate mother, the woman I wanted to grow up to be. She spent her last decades exactly as she had the previous ones; her influence on the rest of us only increased with her age. She was matter-of-fact about her aging, explaining (but not complaining) when first she had to use a walker and later a wheelchair for peace marches and demonstrations. When she was ninety-nine and a half, Muriel reported to me with pleasure that she moved to an "old people's residence"—a.k.a. an assisted-living centre or retirement home—so she didn't have to cook anymore, thus subverting my inherited dread of warehousing. (When I repeated her words to other Halifax friends, they laughed and assured me that Muriel hadn't had to cook for years, as her wide circle of other surrogate daughters had been looking after her carefully.)

In 2005, eighteen years after my last film, I began the film that became SHAMELESS: The ART of Disability. I thought I had left filmmaking behind. I felt old and outdated as a film-maker and a bit scared of exposing myself as a woman aging with disability. But I was living an experience I needed to explore and share, one that resonated with my previous life/ film work around representation and media access.

People with disabilities—like aging people—are either invisible or hypervisible, their/our image distorted by other people's fears. My life, and that of my friends and "rolling-models," was nothing like what we saw in the movies. Several disabled artists agreed to collaborate with me to contradict those negative stereotypes (passive, pitiful, saintly, demonic) and to create authentic representations of our lives, in all their diversity, joy, pain and humour. After all, everyone will become disabled if they're lucky to live long enough. Audiences have responded to SHAMELESS with relief, surprise and even envy at our sense of community.

Disability and aging have a lot of parallels and overlap. What I've learned from living with disability is that it's not the end of the world. To borrow from feminist theory, disability is a social construct as well as a biological one. Society puts obstacles like stairs in front of my scooter; if the stairs weren't there, I would be free to go anywhere. However, obstacles create problems to be resolved; they challenge our creativity and sense of humour. We are forced to create new neural pathways in our brain as we create alternative ways around obstacles. My friends who live with disabilities are among the most resourceful, funny, generous and, yes, brave (although we hate that stereotype too!) people I know. Surprisingly, each of us feels that we're not as disabled as other people with disabilities around us.

Disability is also a head start on conservation—very timely when the planet demands that we learn to live more simply. When our energy is scarce, we learn to conserve for the long haul. I weigh the energy cost of activities, the immediate gratification versus the long-term cost. For example, losing the ability to drive seemed to others—and initially to me—a major blow, a giant step down the steep slope of aging and powerlessness. It's the opposite. It has freed me from mundane tasks like driving to the supermarket or frantic consumerism; I shop locally and choose my medical and personal services within rolling distance of scooter or tricycle. I invite good or would-be friends to my house for tea or potluck instead of going out. I create art with my five-year-old granddaughter like "71 reasons why we love Boppa" for Michael's seventy-first birthday instead of buying a generic card from Hallmark.

The loss of mobility and energy means I'm able to do less— less than I used to, less than most of my age-mates. I have had to learn to value *being* as I previously valued *doing*. This has not been easy for me. I spend a lot of time on the telephone and email, keeping in touch with people who've been part of my life, connecting, remembering, acknowledging. I keep a growing list of friends who are sick or who have lost loved ones. I sign petitions and write politicians. I encourage the work of young filmmakers. Most of all, I make myself available and present to listen. Probably my strength as a documentary filmmaker was the ability to listen well to people's stories.

Currently, I am learning and teaching the skill set known as "Compassionate Listening," a tool for increasing understanding amidst conflict, thus creating a culture of peace. My husband, Michael, and I were part of a Compassionate Listening delegation to Israel and the West Bank and have created an interactive presentation to bring home the first-person stories of Jews and Palestinians. I am finally on my way to becoming a Speaking Our Peace woman as I promised Seth.

People assume I have a particular wisdom that comes from a close encounter with death. Sometimes I think that's laughable; sometimes I admit (or hope) that it is true. Disability does confer a certain kind of wisdom. It is the knowledge of the fragility and randomness of life—like the tragedy that killed my great-niece Miriam. It's appreciating the love of family and friends, the joy of the present moment.

I work to remain conscious of these essential values. Silence helps. Yoga and swimming, too. And most of all, aging. As I watch more friends and family die or develop infirmities, I am brought back to this consciousness.

My post-stroke life has been about balance, metaphorically and physically. And isn't everyone's? Michael and I spent twenty years preventing falls, knowing that I often lose my balance and that a major fracture could destroy my tenuous mobility. So when my hand slid down the door as I was getting out of our van one rainy day last year and I fractured my hip—the "better" one that supports the one more affected by my stroke—I thought it was all over.

After several weeks of post-surgical hospitalization, I was transferred to a "transition unit" for several months of non-weight-bearing recuperation. The first night, I heard blood-curdling howls. The transition unit is located on the first floor of a nursing home; the three floors above house people—mostly women, I was told—at the last stage of their lives. Women like my own mother.

At sixty-seven, I was one of the youngest and, despite my disabilities, the healthiest, on our small ward. Most of the others were transitioning to a placement for people who require more complex care. Many were depressed and scared. My family and friends were horrified by my new surroundings. But since I found myself there, I became an anthropologist of aging.

One of my roommates had broken her shoulder in the most recent of many falls and could not use her walker. She wanted only to go back home to her ninety-one-year-old husband, who could no longer care for her himself. She looked in her mirror and said, "That's not Ruth; that's not me. Ruth is beautiful; she's a well-known ice-skating teacher." Ruth was angry and often nasty to the staff, who tried their best not to reciprocate but were often unsuccessful.

In stark contrast, there was Dorothy—a single Scotswoman, a long-retired physiotherapist apparently legendary for visiting remote outposts in British Columbia. She had a dry sense of humour and no hint of self-pity. Dorothy was totally accepting, but her clear blue eyes told me she knew her days of independent living were limited after she'd broken her leg.

The last of our roommates was seriously misplaced in the transition unit; she was days from death. Beth and her family had long ago decided on a home death, but somehow their family doctor was absent or not consulted. Beth moaned the first few nights in pain and distress, plaintively reciting her street address over and over. After she was properly oxygenated and medicated for her acute pain, she relaxed into a gentle restfulness. She told her family she was ready to die. She was surrounded day and night with loving children, grandchildren and great-grandchildren. Across the room, I wept as Beth's daughter-in-law fed her ice cubes she'd ground in a blender while she wiped her brow and told her how much she loved her.

I am grateful to have had this variety of role models for living with disability, aging and dying. How few conversations we have about death, and how hard we work to avoid and deny it. Surviving my stroke and hip fracture has given me confidence in my own strength and ability to cope and at the same time eliminated the fear of death. I have confronted and accepted my mortality. I don't want to lose intimacy with its imminence.

My mother's biggest fear, and the hardest part of becoming disabled, is becoming dependent on others. I had to learn to ask for the help I need without feeling guilt or shame, in a world that overrates youth and "independence." I've learned that independence is deceptive and illusory. We are interdependent. We are community. I need you and you need me.

In fact, you need me to need you. I've learned that I am performing what we Jews call a *mitzvah* when I give you the opportunity to help me, to be the best and most generous person you can be. I pray that this learning will stay with me and help me share the disabilities that will inevitably accompany my aging.

It is enough.

....

BONNIE SHERR KLEIN *directed award-winning documentary films in the National Film Board's Challenge for Change program and the feminist Studio D, including the infamous* Not a Love Story: A Film about Pornography. *After surviving a brainstem stroke, she wrote* Slow Dance, *co-founded the KickstART! Festival of Disability Art and Culture, and directed* SHAMELESS: The ART *of Disability.*

Knowing

From Zero to Not Quite So Stupid

FRANCES BULA

The nasty parts of old age always poke you so sharply and insistently.

There are often months at a time where I don't wake up without some kind of pain afflicting me before I've even come to full consciousness. A knee that aches from too much walking the day before, a section of spine that feels rigid and bruised. Lately, it's my right shoulder, the side I sleep on. It will pass, I know, only to be replaced by something else.

And then there are the jolts of memory gap, which become memorable in themselves because they're so mortifying. I used to be a whiz, Rainman-like, in my affinity for numbers and my ability to memorize them. Song lyrics, forget it, but I know the social insurance number of my 1977–80 boyfriend and the phone number of the house of my teenage years. Now, I often see a number show up on my BlackBerry screen, and I can feel the aura of the person calling—I know this is a woman, someone I like, someone young—but I can't attach the specific identity anymore. As for remembering people in the flesh, that's become ever more problematic. I find myself having to explain that, after fifty-five years—twenty-five of them as a journalist meeting new people every month—my hard disk is full and that's why I don't remember you (despite how often we've met or how important you are).

If only the good parts of aging produced as distinctive an effect. If only it could happen that every time I did something wise and thoughtful—an act or decision that never would have occurred to my younger self—I'd get a pure blast of some powerful, narcotically uplifting substance through my veins. Instead of that negative jab over the forgotten face or the new persistent body twinge, I'd feel a sense of intense euphoria with each realization that *I am not as f***ing stupid as I used to be*.

Because that's the real payoff of three to four extra decades. Oh, people like to talk about those other pleasures of not being twenty: the financial security, the satisfaction of an interesting career trajectory, the self-acceptance, the rich and stable relationships, the thrill of launching your kids into the world, the remodelled kitchen. But those are the secondary benefits. The real, everyday value of being older is the dozens and dozens of dumb, idiotic, careless, unthinking, didn't-plan-ahead-for-a-second decisions you've accumulated. Those hundreds of mistakes, accompanied during the decades by the gradual realization that you are not the centre of the universe, all start paying dividends as you hit your fifties.

There are people out there who were smarter than I was in my teens and twenties. I see those kinds of young people around even now: bright, young things whose lives are like arrows that fly unerringly towards the bull's eye. They work hard at school, have dozens of great friends, a boyfriend or girlfriend whom they date for years and eventually marry, an interesting job, a house by the time they're thirty, two well-spaced kids shortly after, and even a little fund started for their early retirements.

They do not, as I did, meander through their bachelor's degree studies for almost a decade, dropping abruptly out of fourth year to follow a boyfriend across the country while he shops for a commercial fishing boat. They do not have one explosive relationship after another whose melodramatic crashes and burns (yes, fishing boyfriend among them) at first entertain and then utterly bore their friends. They do not drive death-row cars around town with no brakes, broken ignitions that require hot-wiring to start and holes in the floor. They do not hitchhike across Canada and find themselves detoured one summer afternoon onto a lonely road in a northern Ontario forest with a man who appears to be weighing how much of a fight they'll put up if he attacks.

This is only the beginning of the litany I could recite. I did so many dumb things when I was young that I'm fairly certain I've forgotten most of them. And even the ones I remember fill entire categories: mistakes about relationships, mistakes about money, mistakes about friends, mistakes about family, mistakes about real estate, mistakes at work, mistakes about colleagues...

But I also know I was not totally alone in my ineptitude. There were others all around me doing spectacular belly flops into the ocean of life at the same time. Several quit good jobs in fits of anger. Many drifted along, never really deciding what they wanted to do with their lives, going from one time-wasting job to the next as they talked about studying to do this or that. Another dithered between a girlfriend and a wife for almost a decade from his early twenties to his early thirties, making several people miserable in the process, while another got married on an impulse and was divorced, with a kid to raise on her own, within a couple of years.

And now, with dozens of twenty-somethings in my life through teaching and my six-kid blended, extended family, I see a whole new generation of people struggling to learn life's basic lessons, large and small. Lesson 1: You will need money tomorrow, as well as today, so it's not a bad idea to think about hanging on to at least a little for the next twenty-four hours. Lesson 2: In a European city you're not familiar with, it's good to check to see which airport your plane leaves from so that you don't go to the wrong one. Lesson 3: You can piss off only so many people before you start to run out of friends and places to work. Lesson 4: If you don't take care of your car, it will eventually break down completely—usually when it's most inconvenient—and the repairs will cost you a lot more than they would have if you'd done something at the beginning. Lesson 5: Marriage doesn't solve the problems you think it will. Lesson 6: Everyone says figure out what you want to do and get good at it, but that's hard to do. Lesson 7: No, you're not the only person in the world who just had a HUGE CRISIS and therefore needs to be allowed to blow off all commitments and general standards of civil behaviour.

As I read their emails and texts and Facebook messages— "One of our roommates at the house just gave us notice half-way through the month and said he's not paying the next month's rent. Can he do that?" or "I thought I was his girl-friend when I moved in with him but he says I misunderstood" or "I crashed the car and the other driver says it was my fault. What do I do now?"—I find myself gearing up as usual to help but also feeling an enormous sense of relief at the knowl-edge that I am not ever, ever going to have to go through that kind of painful learning again. Of course, I have other kinds of pain coming in my life, pain that I can't even predict. As much as I'd like the good parts to stay unchanged and the bad parts to improve, experience tells me that's not going to hap-pen. And it's a relief to understand that, too.

Because, as I'd like to say to all of my struggling young friends, eventually it works out. You make all these terrible mistakes or awful things happen to you and you don't han-dle it well, but mostly you come through. I did finish my bachelor's degree, with honours, and got a master's. In spite of two terrible car crashes in my bad-driving days, I lived. Now I drive a van that I maintain religiously. Even though I took any number of truly crazy chances hitchhiking around the world, I didn't get raped, beaten or killed.

And, although it took me until I was twenty-eight, I figured out what I wanted to do with my life. Now I do work that I love, work that makes me wake up happy and energized every day. I've gotten smarter about money; I know the difference between a variable and a fixed mortgage, I miraculously bought a bigger house just before the last doubling of house prices, and my RRSPs are maxed out. And I've shared my life for ten years now with someone, negotiating the ups and downs of everyday life without either one of us having to resort to threats of self-mutilation or flight across the country to make our points. We read the Sunday newspaper together and take turns getting each other breakfast.

But best of all, I'm a kinder, more tolerant person with better judgement about others. I'm both less easily charmed and less harsh when I meet people for the first time. And especially less harsh with those close to me. My mother would tell you that, if she could. She bore the brunt of many of my youthful blunders, lending me money, moving in to help me when I was a single mother, sitting by herself at my university graduation party—the one where I showed up three hours late because I went to another party, got drunk and forgot where I was supposed to be. And she bore the brunt of my rebellion against her.

We did a lot together in that magical preteen period that parents get. I helped her mark homework from the high-school French classes she taught, typed the scripts she wrote for the CBC and listened rapturously to the stories she'd tell at the dinner table about the latest movie she'd seen or book she'd read. I've never seen *A Patch of Blue,* but I remember it vividly from her account.

But then, like the majority of teenagers, I got surly and mean and stopped talking to her as I negotiated my way alone through teenage drinking, boyfriends, breakups and depression. I raged to all my friends about how unfair she was, what a control freak, how she always picked on me to be perfect while my three brothers got away with everything. Although we never stopped talking, our relationship was turbulent and filled with seething resentments on both sides for decades. I was sure that she complained to her friends that I was never going to make anything of myself. And I was alert for any hint of her secret plan to undermine me, raging at her when she said, "You're just like your father" (an alcoholic who died in a Downtown Eastside hotel), when I couldn't get my spending under control or when I overheard her saying to my then-four-year-old, "Oh, too bad your mother went out again without saying goodbye to you."

Our relationship slowly shifted as I got my life in order and as my twenty-something sense of victimization faded. I still got mad at her for her silly, Saskatchewan farm-kid timidness—she felt it was improper to phone her eighty-year-old boyfriend, that he should always phone her—but it was more the exasperation of a friend than an angry daughter. She became an interesting person to me again. I helped edit stories she wrote about her life on the farm during the Depression, and I called her almost every day to talk about everything—from what kind of funeral she wanted ("Do we have to have this discussion first thing in the morning, Mum?") to the play that she and her boyfriend, Walter, had seen that week.

I miss those daily talks now, those few minutes of connection. My mother isn't dead, but she has Alzheimer's. In the first two years after the official diagnosis, we still talked every day. I'd ask her what she remembered about the farm or teaching. And she, trying to show that she was still with it, always asked what all of us were doing—over and over again—which I answered each time. As things got worse and she became more confused and panicky, I'd talk to her to calm her down, tell her to look at all of the pictures of us on the wall.

We still talk, but I have to visit in person because she doesn't know anymore how to use a phone. She's always happy to see me, even if she thinks I'm her sister sometimes, and I'm comforted that she's happy. I sit with her, asking about her day, while other women around me do the same with their mothers who are further along, locked into a world without speech. We all murmur in their ears, tease them, call them Mummy, urge them to eat, become pleased if we can get a smile from them. Getting older seems so lovely then, in its bittersweet way. Yes, we have aching knees or memories that are like a dark night with only occasional flashes of light, but we've learned so much about being kind.

....

FRANCES BULA *is a blogger (www.francesbula.com), veteran reporter on urban issues and columnist for* Vancouver *magazine. Her interests range from how cities work to how we live our lives. Her training included a degree in French literature and working in the commercial fishing industry—two things that taught her everything she needed to know.*

Turkey Flap Wisdom

LYNDSAY GREEN

O ne winter evening some years ago, my teenage daughter and I were soaking together in a backyard hot tub. The moonlight was bright, and I caught her staring at me through the steam. She was looking at me as if seeing me for the first time, and she said, with genuine compassion, "Mom, do you mind growing old?"

I hesitated and then responded with my own question, "How do you feel about how *you* look?" As she made a face and struggled to find the words, I said, "See, you're beautiful and you don't see it. And I'm well past my best-before date, and I think I look great."

She responded with sheer amazement. "You do?"

When the author Annie Dillard was young, she was dismayed to find that her elders were coming apart and seemed neither to notice nor to mind. She was revolted by their deterioration but hid her feelings so as not to be rude. In her essay "An American Childhood," she wondered why they couldn't notice such a "prominent defect" as their "limp, coarse skin" and illustrated the problem using her mother's hand. "I picked up a transverse pinch of skin over the knuckle of her index finger and let it drop. The pinch didn't snap back; it lay dead across her knuckle in a yellowish ridge."

Her mother eventually ended this exploration of her hands with the admonishment, "That's getting boring."

I read this interplay with a laugh of recognition. I have the same response when my daughter amuses herself by playing with my "turkey flap"—her name for the flesh hanging on the underside of my upper arm that has surrendered to gravity. Like Annie's mother, I let my daughter amuse herself for a while before calling a halt to the game. I'm neither offended nor mortified—just bored. Clearly, I'm not taking my breakdown seriously, either.

What accounts for this widely shared disconnect between our appearance and our self-perception as we age? One oft-repeated joke is that our failing eyesight protects us from reality. We can no longer see how far things have fallen. There's some truth to that, but there is also something deeper at work: our expectations have dropped farther than our flesh.

I'm grateful that most body parts still work, and I've lived long enough to know that the present state sure beats the alternative. How could I bemoan my saggy bits when friends have lopped off parts and excavated organs to fight to stay alive? How could I not be grateful to my body for continuing the good fight—in whatever form—thinking about my friends who died too young? They would have made Faustian bargains for this chance to have their wrinkled body scrutinized by their glowing-skinned offspring. So I rejoice at still being here, imperfect as I am, to be played with by my beautiful daughters.

It turns out that this sunny thought process is, itself, a function of aging. While our bodies are deteriorating, our brains are helping us cope. Research studies consistently find that older people are better able to manage their emotions than younger people. One of the explanations that rings true for me is that we are more likely than our younger counterparts to have mixed emotions. Things become less black and white.

For me, having children was the point at which I stopped feeling the pure emotions of joy and sorrow: everything became bittersweet. I would rejoice in being awarded a new business contract but saddened, realizing it would take time away from my family. I would relish my place on the pedestal of wisdom when my daughters were young, at the same time anticipating and mourning the inevitable tumble I would take from the perch. My delight in spending time with them was coupled with the sorrow of knowing that some day they would leave me to launch their own lives.

Apparently, having these mixed emotions and avoiding the extremes allow us to manage stress better and help us recover more quickly from adversity. Neuroscientists can now watch this process on brain scans. Researchers in Wisconsin, for example, identified a group of older adults who regulated their emotions effectively and studied their brain activity. Unlike others with less emotional control, this group used their prefrontal cortex to rein in the amygdala, which processes stressful emotions like fear and anxiety.

Our emotional maturity means that we don't take offence as easily as young people. Another study in California subjected younger and older adults to personal criticism and then asked them to report their thoughts and emotions. Whereas the younger adults dwelled on the negative comments and demanded more details, the older adults were less likely to focus on the negative. Thinking back to my hot tub discussion, the younger me could easily have taken offence at my daughter's pointed question. I might have grilled her about exactly which body parts led her to think I was past my prime and insisted she identify the telltale signs. I could have made her very sorry she'd ever brought up the subject. But, now, as with Annie's mother, it's hard to get a rise out of me.

At times like this, I am glad to be getting old. I like the way I think, and I'm not alone. Provided we don't have dementia, the older we get, the happier we get, despite the accompanying deterioration of our bodies! Stats Canada research has found that nearly two-thirds of people over eighty-five report that they're in good to excellent health. They persist in this belief even though they probably have at least one chronic condition, including arthritis and rheumatism, high blood pressure, back problems, heart disease, as well as vision and hearing problems. Here is living proof that, at a certain point, "still breathing" is a cause for celebration.

In the past, younger people could more easily seek out this wise world view of their elders. Their grandparents lived nearby, if not under the same roof, and elderly relatives and friends were part of religious and social activities. Now we're much more likely to be gathered in age silos that isolate generations one from another.

To remedy this, young people are beginning to use the Internet in ingenious ways to connect with the wisdom of their elders. A website called Elder Wisdom Circle links "cyber-grandparents" across North America with people in their teens, twenties, thirties. More than six hundred elders respond to online requests for advice with confidential and personal guidance. Topics cover the range of life's challenges. A twenty-two-year-old asks whether she needs to invite her husband's ex-girlfriend to her baby shower, as he would like. The elder's response supports the young woman's instincts and provides an example from the older woman's own life by way of reinforcement. In another letter, a sixteen-year-old asks, "Do you have any advice on just life in general?" The writer (gender not specified) is doing well in school but feels unmotivated and pressured by parents to make decisions about the future. The letter concludes, "This may not seem like much of a problem *per se*, but I just feel confused about pretty much the rest of my life and how to get there." The elder's response is the perfect combination of acknowledgement, personal examples and reassurance.

Also delightful is a blog called "Life Advice from Old People," where Seth Menachem posts videos of old people giving advice. What they have to say is touching and wise. We get to watch one elder as he fulfills his dream at the age of ninety-two of hitting a ball at Fenway Park. Preparing for the big day, he says, "My strategy is to... do the very best I possibly can. I'm sure I'll be a little nervous when I step up to the plate. But it's just one of those things you have to face in life—whether you're playing baseball, going to a dance or performing on stage." Another video features Farmer Tom, who started his life over and became a cattle farmer at sixty-five. Now seventy, he encourages us to keep moving. "Keep doing new things. You have plenty of time to rest when you're dead."

I, too, decided to seek wisdom from the elders. After spending countless hours in retirement homes and care facilities with my long-living relatives, I realized I needed help. It dawned on me that I could well live a long life, and I felt inadequate to the task. Finding that others shared my concern, I decided to write a guidebook; I sought out seniors who were successfully navigating the terrain of old age to be my guides and asked them what I should be doing to prepare.

To find these role models, I asked friends and acquaintances, "Who do you want to be when you grow up?" The forty seniors we identified resided in seven cities across Canada, ranged in age from seventy-five to one hundred and came from a broad spectrum of education and income levels. During the several hours of intimate conversation I shared with each of them, I listened to their advice and heard their stories. To encourage candour, I promised to disguise their identities in the book.

I composed questions asking what advice the seniors received when they were younger that was helping them now, which of their strengths made it easier to be old, which weaknesses made it harder and what I should be doing now to prepare for a potentially long life. Before the interview process began, I showed my questionnaire to a young psychiatrist. "You should ask them what is good about being old," she advised. I agreed that would make a really good addition and turned the question to her: "What do *you* think is good about being old?" Her reply shocked me. "Nothing," she said, "Not a single thing."

I was relieved to find that the elders didn't share her perspective. On the contrary, old age has brought them many advantages. For one thing, their worries have been reduced. Since they are no longer in the thick of things, life has become less stressful. As one of them put it, "I'm not really competing with anyone for anything."

Also, they find they have developed a certain equanimity— there are those mixed emotions we talked about earlier. "If you've managed to get this far along, you don't worry so much. Even though you can't do all the things you used to be able to do, what you manage to do can be equally satisfying."

Another advantage of old age is more control over one's time. As you get older, you realize that time is a precious commodity, and you stop squandering it on things that are low priority. "You are mistress of your fate," one elder puts it. "You do what you want, and you don't do what you don't want."

The elders find that one of the most powerful prerogatives of age is permission to speak the truth. Simone de Beauvoir says that this privilege results from society's rejection of old people. Since they have been "relegated to the fringe of humanity," they no longer have to please others. This position brings a measure of *grey power*, which has been harnessed so effectively by groups like the Gray Panthers and the Raging Grannies to battle for social change.

But what about the deteriorating appearance that so disconcerts young people? Elders report that a decline in youthful good looks is offset by an acceptance of self. As one said, "When I look in the mirror, I talk to myself. I have scars, and my formerly curly hair is now straight. I say to myself, 'So, you're not beautiful—you're not having to please anyone but yourself. You are what you are.' "

The elders I spoke with were too modest to say that age had given them wisdom, but they know they've acquired lots of experience—which can look like the same thing. As one woman observed, "I have gained my authority from having lived so much. I really do know better."

Although our bodies may leave something to be desired, what's in our heads remains much in demand. Annie Dillard admits that in contrast to her elders', her youthful beauty had its limits. "Our beauty was a mere absence of decrepitude; their beauty, when they had it, was not passive but earned; it was grandeur; it was a party to power, and to artifice, even, and to knowledge."

So those aren't wrinkles you see on my face—they're lines of knowing. As for the turkey flaps, that's where I store my wisdom.

LYNDSAY GREEN *has spent her career helping people use communications technologies for learning. Her book,* You Could Live a Long Time: Are You Ready? *(Thomas Allen Publishers, 2010), provides advice from elders to boomers. Her conclusion: we should stop fighting to stay young and embrace aging.*

It's All Fine

LAURA ROBIN

It's an unseasonably cool late-August morning. I'm snuggled down in my sleeping bag in the bunkhouse at Kathee's cottage. Outside, in the still, silent morning, mist is hovering over the silvery lake.

"The mist in your hair! Come get the mist in your hair!" Charlotte is grinning impishly and wiggling her fingers above her head to demonstrate.

Soon, there are eight or ten of us in the lake, gliding around in the soft water, never quite reaching the mist. And I'm just so happy and grateful to be with these women, to be one of these women.

I feel rich in the presence of my women friends—sparkling like a small constellation all around me.

There are lots of things I don't like about being fifty-something: that shrewish look I get around my mouth when I'm being judgemental or when I'm merely tired, losing my reading glasses all over the house, the indignity of my bum sagging.

But if I weren't fifty, these wonderful women wouldn't be my friends. And I wouldn't trade them for 20/20 vision or a tight butt—not for an instant.

The women here at the cottage are members of my book club—a dozen of us whose connection goes back two decades to a neighbourhood playgroup. Twenty years ago, we were pouring apple juice, wiping noses and reading picture books aloud. Now we're sipping wine, sharing menopause remedies and widening our view of the world discussing books.

On this watery morning, while most of us are swimming, others are inside the cottage setting out homemade granola, baking orange-cranberry scones and brewing coffee and chai. Really, does life get any better?

There always seems to be someone who has already gone through whatever you're facing next. From these women, I've learned that paying for a perfectly good and perfectly empty apartment each summer your child is home from McGill University is to be expected, that rooibos tea tastes way better with honey and milk and that you can balance an egg on its end at the equinox (apparently—this one I've taken on faith).

From other women, I've learned how comforting it is to have a friend who will walk with you and listen when you're flying apart because a parent is dying, how to slide even spelt-flour pastry off the counter and into a pie plate and what is the right way to behave if your husband leaves you.

Some women say it's the fuck-you fifties.

A hairdresser I know told me he was putting on a course to teach stylists how to handle the fifty-year-old client.

"So we need some kind of special handling?" I said, bristling (and pretty much answering my own question).

I acknowledge that some of us, some of the time, have a certain unwillingness to put up with crap. Okay, maybe that's most of us most of the time. We're less willing to accept stupid comments, unnecessary procedure for procedure's sake or chirpy, insincere patter.

Biting our tongue, obsequiousness, even flirtatiousness—things that might have seemed to serve us well at a younger age—now seem like a betrayal of who we are. Most of my favourite women are shockingly direct. And funny.

So I acknowledge the argument for the fuck-you fifties. But I think an equal case can be made for the all-fine fifties.

I went to Paris for the first time after I turned fifty. The idea of jumping at an airline seat sale (that night, before midnight!) came up at a book-club meeting. Three of us signed on. And, later, so did Helen, my rarely seen best friend from childhood, who now lives in London.

On the morning we arrived in Paris, as we three from Ottawa pulled our suitcases along the cobbled *rue*, searching the giant doors for our rented address, I vaguely noticed another woman walking towards us. On some less-than-conscious level, I assumed she was a local but noticed she was about our age and felt some sense of recognition, some immediate friendliness towards her. It turned out to be Helen.

We four had no agenda, no must-see list, and spent four fabulous days. Whatever we did, wherever we ended up, seemed to be just fine for everyone.

On our last night, we took the evening dinner boat tour on the Seine. It was predictably touristy but fun, complete with a singer who sang "Purple Rain" with a Parisian accent. (I'd never understood the appeal of that song before, but I loved it that night.)

When we left our table to wander out on the deck to get some fresh air and a better view, an American woman about our age joined us.

"I'm with a bus tour," she said. "I didn't think I was at the bus-tour stage, but apparently I am."

We chatted awhile, and the conversation turned to the relatively new twinkling lights on the Eiffel Tower. Helen and Kathee are architects, and they debated whether the lights were a tacky distraction on the elegant structure or added welcome sparkle to the Parisian night.

I asked the American woman what she thought.

"It's fine," she said contentedly. "It's all just fine."

Later, I recounted this story to my friend Susan—the one who knows how to behave when your husband leaves you—and it delighted her, too. Because at fifty-something, we are finally starting to realize that when it comes to most stuff—whether we go to this restaurant or that one, whether the leaves get raked today or next week, whether to keep getting your hair dyed or go grey—it's all just fine. Susan and I have now made "it's all fine" something of a mantra.

Most of the year, I'm fortunate enough to be able to ride my bike to work, and my route home takes me beside a river. Most men I pass on the bike path have their heads down and seem serious about their cycling. Some women do, too. But, often, especially at the end of the day, I'll look up to see a woman of a certain age cycling towards me, or strolling on the path, and we look each other in the eye. And we smile. And although we're complete strangers, we feel an essential recognition.

It reminds me of the salutation "Namaste" said at the end of many yoga classes. The simple translation is "I bow to you," though one yoga teacher I know offers a more eloquent version, from Mahatma Gandhi:

> I honour the place in you where the entire universe resides. I honour the place in you of light, love, truth, peace and wisdom. I honour the place in you where, when you are in that place, and I am in that place, there is only one of us.

Or maybe, for me and the women on the bike path, it could be "I honour the place in you of grey roots, family responsibilities, sagging butts, friendship and laughter. And when you are on this path, and I am on this path, we share the same fresh air and beautiful view.

"And it's all just fine."

....

LAURA ROBIN *is a journalist at the* Ottawa Citizen. *She has won numerous awards for writing and editing in her current role as editor of the travel section.*

The Joys of Mostly
Good Enough

HEATHER-JANE ROBERTSON

*D*oes aging feel great, or is it just *supposed* to feel great? Is pro-aging propaganda just one demographic click away from those nice little pamphlets that proclaimed "It's Wonderful to Become a Woman!"? "Have a happy period" and "Have a happy bladder leak" share a spooky resemblance that I have trouble ignoring. Are we afraid that just as each of us failed to play the perfect roles of dutiful daughter, supportive wife, transformational leader, woman-who-has-it-all, we may find that we're not even doing "old" as well as we're supposed to?

My internal jury (composed of not only me, myself and I but also my mother, Gloria Steinem and Miss Gold, my first home ec teacher) seems hopelessly deadlocked on whether or not I can genuinely embrace this theme.

On the one hand (that would be the one with less arthritis but more age spots), parts of aging are good, or mostly good. There is the paradox of time, in that it is abundant in the present but increasingly scarce in the future. Unlike many of my similarly aged friends who claim never to have been so busy or overscheduled, I have never had so few things on my list that need to be done today, right this minute, so that the next thing can follow. There are, indeed, many things to do, read, write, draw, consider, but there is substantial freedom in knowing that very little will happen if they aren't done until tomorrow. On the other hand, very little will happen if they aren't done at all, and that rubs.

But not as hard as might be expected. The sting of guilt, once so sharp, becomes duller and sillier. It seems to me that advancing age is, by and large, incompatible with most of our more common and corrosive failings and neuroses, and that should be a good thing, yes? Narcissists soon learn that although co-workers might once have tolerated a self-absorbed albeit productive or powerful colleague, the post-employment world doesn't cut much slack for people who expect it to be all about them. Folks who at one time found dealing with you irritating but necessary can become folks who don't have to bother dealing with you at all.

Vanity—the idea that people admire you (when they actually prefer themselves)—is also hard to sustain, thanks to the many people determined to undermine any display of high self-regard. (Yes, girly, I mean you, rolling your eyes dramatically as an older woman with an unfortunate fondness for bronzing products and leopard prints wanted your attention at the cosmetics counter yesterday. I know, I know, she seemed to think you were employed for that very purpose. I gather that selling anti-aging products to people who actually need them, and can even afford them, is oh so icky.)

Which leads me to one of the vices aging doesn't seem to vanquish—not just bitchiness, but a particular kind of unrepentant bitchiness. I realize my tone of voice was a tad aggressive when I informed the clerk that yes, that ridiculous, shrunken excuse for a nightgown had been hand-washed in cold water. (Thank you, Miss Gold, grade eight home ec.) But remarking that I had been washing "dainties" for a decade or two before the clerk (and perhaps her mother) were born was both gratuitous and ineffective. I pointed out, somewhat shrilly, that her store's policy of refunding the purchase price of items that shrank only if they hadn't been washed was oxymoronic. No, I did not call her a moron—which was what she heard, of course—but I didn't bother clearing up the confusion, either. This, I admit, is unapologetic bitchiness.

Perhaps I would behave this way more often if I could be guaranteed an audience that would be either suitably shocked or duly impressed when I told my stories. What is the point of cultivating a dragon lady persona if every woman to whom you recount your latest anecdote would have behaved at least as badly, or perhaps worse? Outrageousness among my contemporaries is so commonplace that we no longer shock each other in the retelling of our adventures; these merely provide openings for more shared hilarity.

In fact, laughter, more than anything else, is what replaces the joys of things lost and makes the joys of things found richer, wider, deeper. Once I imagined my old-lady future as featuring a rocking chair on the front porch, unlimited butter tarts to eat and a microphone through which I could bombast neighbours and passers-by on the evils of capitalism, misogyny and pantyhose. The impulse to act out this scenario is still present, but now I know that I would be unable to restrain my impulse to laugh as well as rant, entirely spoiling the effect.

I have it on good report that there are female paragons among us who eat nothing but locally sourced fibre and drink only free-range herbal teas. These are wise crones, the hearts and souls of their families and communities. They channel compassion, speak infrequently but with great probity, and attract others with their constancy. They model for pro-aging advertising campaigns, wear white linen shirts to the market (even in winter), adore (but never boast about) their organically raised grandchildren. Spiritually grounded, they often hold hands with men with full heads of hair and enjoy long walks on the beach without any thought about the location of public washrooms. They never leave home without SPF 75, they eschew red meat, and (as a consequence) they will be very well preserved both before and after death.

I confess I have not met any members of this incarnation of Stepford Sisterhood, but they must exist: countless books and magazines advise me of how to join their ranks. Through the media, we are still urged, as we have been since girlhood, to strive to be "better" by being less like ourselves. This decade around, the injunctions are different but no less unnatural: we are told we can be timeless, gravity defying, purged of our toxins/toxicity. Is this about fear of infirmity and death, or is it a fear of women and nature?

I do find it ironic that menopause is commonly referred to as "the change"—as if before was one thing, and after yet another. Many years after we supposedly "changed," I have to report that my friends and I still seem pretty much ourselves; mostly our virtues and vices are neither particularly evolved nor suddenly dissolute. Day after day, we are who we were, and that seems mostly good enough.

Perhaps this is the phrase that our generation of women might consider claiming as our own: Mostly Good Enough. I think it's a concept that my six-member internal jury could live with. It's versatile, in that it can describe a day, a life or a haircut. It leaves room for both error and improvement without requiring immediate action on either count. If it is a tad too unambitious and uncommercial for the Stepford crowd (or the media who invented them), let them eat seaweed sushi.

....

HEATHER-JANE ROBERTSON *is a recovering writer, educator, public speaker, activist and friend of unlost progressive causes. Her optimism peaks on Thursdays.*

No Country for Old Women?

LILLIAN ZIMMERMAN

Recently, I gave a talk to a national gerontology organization in London, Ontario, titled *The New Ageisms: No Country for Old Women*. Pretty jazzy, I thought, given my focus on the invisibility of older women and the then popularity of the movie *No Country for Old Men*. But when I arrived at the lecture hall, the sign on the door read *The New Ageisms: No Country for Old Men*. Somebody had decided I'd made an error and then "corrected" it for me. I was not amused.

The signmaker's chutzpah rankled. And it reminded me of Betty Friedan's compelling 1993 book, *The Fountain of Age*. In it, she discusses the "longevity revolution," particularly that of women, who now live to be over eighty-two years. Men, in contrast, top out at around seventy-seven. (This, in turn, reminded me of an article I'd read about an incident at some seniors' group meeting, where a male audience member stood up to complain about this. "The reason men don't live as long as women," he said, "is because the women don't take good enough care of us." There was no mention in the article of how many of the women present snorted with derision.)

Friedan argued that assuming productive life ends at age sixty-five is a myth, because women live at least twenty or more years, occupying a whole new social stage of life. She calls older women "biological pioneers"—a term I love and have adopted for myself. Although Friedan pointed this out almost twenty years ago, we still consider sixty-five the gate-post to old age.

On some level, my experience with the anonymous title-changer symbolizes the cultural gap between this outdated myth and the more recent reality in which women's lives keep growing and developing. But my resentment of the assumption that I'd made a mistake provoked me to find a whole new approach to discussing older women. My take is emphatically contrary to the continuous gloom and doom emphasis on the horrors of aging—especially for women.

Yes, I am familiar with unhappy physical and mental declines, but we're not all dancing down the road to dementia. Very far from it: many of us now occupying this new social stage of life are doing so with verve and passion. In my own circle of older women alone, five of us—including three octogenarians—published books in 2009 on topics ranging from human sexuality to the 1970s "back to the land" experience, for audiences as diverse as older women, cooking enthusiasts and teenagers.

Perhaps because of the general invisibility of older women, it's ironic that we know more about women historically than we do about those who are currently making history. But they are role models for the aging boomer women they precede.

Gloria Steinem, who turned seventy-five in 2009, says it's time for older women—the biological pioneers among whom I count myself—to engage in "speakouts" about their lives.

So here are mine, about the positive qualities of being an older woman:

I have a sense of well-being, a synthesis of lifelong experience that fills me with remarkable and unexpected strength.

I'm more confident now than I have ever been. This outlook is likely based on both professional and personal accomplishments. I was a single parent years before the phrase was invented and successfully raised two terrific boomer women. And I've reinvented myself several times since.

At age thirty-nine, I transformed myself from a working woman to a "grade junkie" university student, where I experienced major cognitive dissonance. Immediately upon graduating, I morphed into a faculty member at a B.C. college, where I honed my professional skills for twenty years. The next transition was a short-lived retirement (I couldn't stand it), after which I became engaged in gerontology. Recently, I've become an author.

In the process, I've learned to make decisions much more quickly and easily—and they're usually good ones.

I'm less defensive than I used to be, probably because I've been able to get rid of the internalized inferiority acquired while growing up female. That assertiveness training that was big in the 1970s? It definitely works. I have stopped saying "I'm sorry" a thousand unnecessary times—when someone bumps into me, for instance!

I find it easier to say no—which wasn't an option when I was growing up. I was socialized to please everybody else, make sure they came first in a world where girls and women came last. But these days, when I go to a restaurant alone, there's no more docile acceptance of a lousy table near the washrooms or kitchens. And when I'm travelling and the occupant of the seat next to me falls asleep with his head lolling onto my shoulder, my silent discomfort has been replaced with a gentle jab in the ribs and a request to "please move."

My personal assertiveness is reflected more broadly in a new phenomenon that's now being referred to as the "grey divorce." Baby boomer women are deciding they want to be independent during their longevity and are leaving marriages in their fifties and sixties—some even in their seventies. This was unthinkable for my generation, in which many women endured unhappy and repressive relationships till death did them part. Now it is more like "till stress do them part."

Recently, I've found that there is a strong but not sufficiently well-known "old girls' network." Not the "old boys' network" of power and elitism but a generous and empowering one. It was of unfathomable assistance when writing my recent book cataloguing my resentment of the invisibility of older women writ large. I cold emailed women across the country for assistance and always got it when it was available.

I am also wallowing in the riches of being a grandmother to adult grandchildren. One is a deep-sea fishing guide, one is a marketing director for a major restaurant chain, and another attends school on a golf scholarship. They have brought whole new worlds to me. (They also crack me up. When my nineteen-year-old grandson graduated from busboy to server, he had to learn how to advise diners on what wine to order. He knew boom-all about wines and hated the ritual of uncorking bottles at the table, which he did badly. His solution? He memorized all the screw-topped wines on the list and suggested them!)

Women's friendships are an unheralded strength at all stages of life, but among older women, they're especially straightforward: no artifices or game playing. It's so relaxing and comfortable to be with peers who have the commonality of many years behind us. When I organized focus groups as research for my book, a number of women spoke about belonging to a "bridge club," where they never play bridge but just get together to talk. Women are, indeed, "fluent in the language of friendship." Have you ever noticed two older women, strangers to one another, passing each other at a mall or on the sidewalk? They give each other a small smile of recognition, as if to say, "We belong to the same club." Whenever I do so, it's always reciprocated.

Older women also boast a distinctive sense of humour. While I was at dinner with a couple of boomer pals in their early sixties recently, the talk turned to ads in women's magazines years ago. We laughed about the "tattletale grey" and "whiter than white" slogans that used to urge women to use a particular brand of soap. We recalled the absurdities offered in advice columns that recommended a woman greet her tired husband with a perfectly mixed martini when he arrived home at the end of the day—or wrap her nude body in cellophane. (Could I make this up?) Well into the wine, one of my dinner companions described her own attempt to jumpstart her dwindling sex life by donning stilettos, fishnet stockings, a sequined bikini and a jewelled headband. Leaning provocatively against the living room door frame where Hubby was in his usual after-dinner mode, stretched out on the couch behind his newspaper, she "ahemed" to get his attention. Down came the paper; he looked her over, said, "Jesus Christ" and returned to his reading. The story made us all howl.

I don't like the currently popular mantra about sixty being the new fifty, eighty being the new seventy and so on. We *are* different from our mothers and grandmothers, but the mantra is ageist; it implies that being fifty is better than being sixty… What's wrong with being sixty—then *or* now? From my informed perspective, being eighty actually has a few advantages over fifty.

Consider, for example, what happened immediately after the invisible helper in London "corrected" the title of my lecture. While I gave my talk, my granddaughter—in her fourth year at the University of Western Ontario at the time—sat in the audience, hanging on to my every word.

It just doesn't get any better than that.

LILLIAN ZIMMERMAN, *a long-time research associate with the Gerontology Research Centre at Simon Fraser University, has spent her career focusing on women's issues. She has written, lectured and made radio and TV appearances. Her book* Baglady or Powerhouse? A Roadmap for Midlife (Boomer) Women *was published in 2009 to favourable reviews.*

Honouring

It Will Be Easy
(and other poems)

SUSAN MCMASTER

I began writing these poems about eight years ago, when I first became aware of a change in my mother's relationship with the world. Since then, Betty Isabelle Emily Page has been diagnosed with Alzheimer's disease. She continues, however, to live independently in her own studio apartment and to engage in many activities, including participating in a study of memory disorders. Betty recently turned eighty-two and is the matriarch of a family of six children and their spouses, fifteen grandchildren and six great-grandchildren. She is currently planning her next twenty years.

I didn't want these poems to go out into the world without her blessing and her voice. Her reaction to publication—repeated many times over several months—was "Great; this is a good time to write poems about this because there are so many old people these days—it'll make them feel less alone." When I read the poems to her, I noted down her comments, which appear in italics. With Betty's permission, I have included a number of these responses, as well as some of her more general comments.

IT WILL BE EASY

I worry a lot about her dying
these days, not so much
about her, how she feels
or will feel
about her death.
I hope it will be easy,
simple as forgetting.
That she'll lie down one evening
and like the rain streaming down
the windows tonight,
just runnel away,
asleep
and snoring maybe
and then
not.

I'd give her this if I could, but still
I'm not worried about her.

If there's nothing, she may be
relieved to give way
to the sleep she always needed
when too many children called.

If there's a heaven, she'll be there,
though they may make her do the dishes.

If it's Nirvana, she'll be bored.
Set out to raise Cain.

*It's very frustrating. Sometimes not even frustrating because I
can't remember what it's all about. So then I don't worry about
it. Just look at what's happening right here and right now.*

CROSSING ARCS

"Don't be ridiculous,
it's far too big for me."

I hold the bathing suit
up to my chest
and see she's right.

Somehow we've slipped
along crossing arcs
as I curve into middle age,
she slides into old.

I pull the suit on.
Have to yank and pull.

The one I've given her
gapes at the legs,
sags at the waist.

In the water, I pause as we
splash through the shallows.
Reach for her hand.

*It's living in the now—it's a pocket memory. I know I'm here
because you're here.*

SURVIVAL

"I'm going to move to a retirement home.
I've had enough."

We've been mentioning the idea
for months—showing her ads—
but it's she who decides, her own decision,
made all in one day.

"Right now. I don't want to ever carry
bags up steps again. Take out the garbage.
Shovel snow from the walk.
I don't want to cook even one more meal."

She doesn't have to think about it.
Something inside, some careful wary beast
watches all the time.

Watches out for itself.
For her, its lair.

Sometimes I feel like a spent volcano.

ORIENTEERING
She's figured it out
with her Girl Guide compass.
Where the doors go,
how the walls fit.
Marked her table
with a line pointing north.

She's met the man down the hall
who calls if she doesn't turn up
for breakfast or lunch, ·
meets her downstairs for a walk by the river.
'Serves her Scotch in a tiny glass.

His name is Bill.
They play billiards together.
Name and game together
easier to remember.
"Sometimes I give him
a hug. That's all.
None of that other stuff."

One day, they start singing
in the Bistro, against the rules,
and everyone joins in.

Now the "I-Can't-Singers"
meet every week
wherever they choose.

*A lot of the stuff that's come and gone is gone, and what you're
left with is what you basically are.*

FACTS
I am imagining myself old
because she's not what she was.
I haul my five decades hand by hand up the stairs,
listen anxiously to my heart beat,
shy away from salt and sugar,
lie late into the day,
wondering how many
more I have left.

This is not what she does.
Faced by clear decay
in a diminished, sunless space,
she covers the walls with her paintings,
the shelves with her pottery and books,
grabs every bit of life that blunders her way.

"My grandmother lived to a hundred and three."

This is not true, but what use are facts?

This is now. As I said, what else can I do?

SIGN OF RESPECT

Afraid she's fallen or had a stroke
when she doesn't answer my knock,
I have the nurse unlock her door,
ignoring with a daughter's disdain
the clearly written Post-it Note—
"Do Not Disturb"
in her school-teacher hand—
stuck above the knob,

and can only laugh
with surprise and a kind of
relief and delight
to see two bare bodies
half rise on the bed,
as I step in.

"Sorry—" I back out fast.

Who gave me the right
to breach a shut door?

What made me sure
age had smothered that flame?

*I may be losing my memory, but it's a discriminating memory.
I have things you will never know—no matter what I remember
or forget. There are places in my mind where you can never go.*

COMFORT

The novels I read
close comfort around me.

The poems I write
scratch trails through my gut
like a cat who's swallowed
a thread of wire
and tries to tooth it out.

"Isn't that what poetry
is supposed to do?" she says.
"Enlighten, point out,
sharpen perception?"

This is a failing mind?

In my room and hers
books cover the floor.

*One good thing—I love reading. I read a book a day. And then
I finish the book and close it, and say to myself, I wonder what
that was all about? So I read it again. Means I can read every
book five times.*

....

SUSAN MCMASTER *is the author or editor of twenty-one books
and recordings, recently* Paper Affair: Poems Selected and
New *(2010) and* Crossing Arcs: Alzheimer's, My Mother, and
Me *(2009), both from Black Moss. She founded* Branching
Out, *the first national feminist magazine, and performs with
Geode Music & Poetry.*

Kick the Can

SHEILA DEANE

The young woman who worked in the tack shop was moving to another city to do graduate research, and her parents told her to get rid of all her animals before she left. She asked me if I wanted her pet chickens so that they wouldn't end up in a stew pot. "Do they lay eggs?" I asked. "Well, not regularly anymore. They're mature hens. The youngest is the rooster." "I don't think I want the rooster." "Oh, you need him. He protects the hens from danger and rounds them up at night. Besides, if you have fertile eggs, you can incubate them next spring and have a new generation of young hens."

I didn't care about the eggs. I wanted the chickens to clean up my mid-summer vegetable garden, eat the squash bugs and slugs. They did that beautifully and earned my admiration—even the rooster, who really did turn out to be essential for the hens' security. His name was Monk, so I christened the chicken coop "Monk's House" and, in what I thought was a clever literary allusion, proceeded to name the hens after Bloomsbury women: Virginia, Vita, Vanessa and Ottoline.

Sometimes when you name an animal for witty, rather than perceptive, reasons, it chucks off its name and suggests another. That was so with Vita, the smallest and oldest, a dappled grey Dorking hen that preferred the name Gracie. Dorking is a breed introduced to England by the Romans; not surprising that some ancient traits remain. The other hens went into the nesting box to lay an egg, then, deed done, got off and went straight back to the vegetable garden. But Gracie kept sitting on her egg and made little mewling noises when I reached under to take it away. One morning, I was cleaning stalls and caught her sneaking out from behind a stack of hay bales. There she had hidden three secret small white eggs. I had to throw them out because I didn't know how old they were, but a few days later there were two more.

I was in the full throes of menopause that summer. Didn't want to do hormone replacement therapy like my mother did. I figured this body used to chug along just fine before it was fuelled by estrogen; surely it could figure out how to do that again. But this was my second year of sleepless nights and painful hot flashes, and I was getting discouraged.

"She's having a last kick at the can," I said, feeling empathy with the old hen who wanted to brood her eggs, so I moved her two eggs from behind the hay bales into the nesting box and showed her where they were. She settled in immediately, flouncing her feathers around them, snuggling her warm breast against them, and began a thirty-day sit.

Occasionally, another hen came into the coop and laid an egg, then, mindful of its career (eating slugs and squash bugs) got up and left. Gracie would look at the other hen's egg, gradually cooling off, and very carefully (thinking what? I wondered) rolled it into her own nest. Did she understand that what she didn't rescue would end up as breakfast? Eventually, she had seven eggs under her, some small and white, some medium light brown, some large and mocha brown.

"Why are you letting her sit? It's too late in the year. You'll have scrawny little things running around freezing to death." That was what my neighbour thought of Gracie's nest. I responded, defensively. "She wants to sit." He countered, like teacher to student. "Take the eggs away. She'll get over it. She's a chicken." I took a deep breath and made a fool of myself. "Well, I think if you're going to keep an animal, because it suits you, because you need it, because you're exploiting it for some reason, it's still entitled to some level of self-determination, whatever you can reasonably manage. Gracie wants to sit, and it's her choice."

I brought her treats—crumpled oat cakes, sunflower seeds, clusters of wild grapes—because she wouldn't leave the coop and I worried she wasn't getting enough food value in the bowl of chicken scratch. I had to lift her off the nest, and she shuddered with those low, mewling cries, as if she were possessed, but when I put her down in front of the treats, she ate with a rapacious appetite, little grunts between each bite. While she ate, I gently picked up each egg and held it to my ear to listen. The books said you could hear the little peeps, and the mother hen would rearrange the eggs in the nest according to how loud the peeps were, cooling and slowing down the more developed, warming and speeding up the less developed, so that they would all hatch on the same day.

I wasn't just Gracie's fool. I knew I was more invested in her eggs than I should be because I was missing my own reproductive years. They call menopause a "change" of life, but that summer, it just felt like loss. The abdomen that had housed my growing babies had gone slack, the breasts that had nursed them were sagging, the arms that had slung them up for a ride on my shoulders were weakening, and even the mind that had soaked up and cherished every moment of their life was becoming forgetful. The physical comforts of their babyhood, the spontaneous fun of their school years, the demanding and transformative challenges of their adolescence: that was all behind me now.

Gracie's most exciting adventure was with a mink. Sunroom windows were open, so from inside the house I could hear the great hullabaloo of chicken outrage and ran top speed to the barn. Outside the coop, the rooster and hens were raising the alarm; inside the coop, Gracie was in a standoff with a beautiful and determined mink. He wanted the eggs; Gracie was not budging. The neighbour said I should have hit him on the head with a shovel. But I couldn't do that. First, he was too gorgeous. Second, it occurred to me that he might be a she, with a litter of mink kittens in need of an omelette. I just shooed her away with a manure fork and hoped she wouldn't come back. And I began locking Gracie in during the days so that she wouldn't be vulnerable. I figured we had only about ten days to go before the little peeps hatched and all would be well.

A few of Gracie's own eggs cracked during her sit. The shells were too thin and brittle, her being older, I guess, and a few mornings I had to clean up the sticky yellow mess in the nest and dab her breast feathers with a warm washcloth. I found it puzzling that there was nothing like a little embryo in the mess.

What compensates for the loss of your reproductive years? Well, lots, but it's more abstract, less sensual. Not singing him lullabies, your hand enfolding and intertwining with his small fingers, but the happiness of his number on call display, his voice, his stories. Not the palpable joy when you turn and see her on top of a mountain of shopping plaza snow, standing in wonder, as if she were on top of Everest, but the email full of travel photos that take all afternoon to download.

At twenty-three days, I began to suspect that Gracie's eggs were duds. I let her be for another week, in case the later stolen eggs were holding things up, but at thirty days, I was ready to give up. While she ate her treat, I mustered the courage to gently shake her eggs. All of them sounded like a little watery milkshake. So. They weren't chicks. They were infertile eggs, and she'd been wasting her time for a whole month. I blamed the rooster.

I took Gracie's eggs away and put them in the refrigerator. I would crack them open in a few days and find that they were all green and rotten. But even with no eggs in the nest, Gracie kept on sitting. In the morning, when I opened the coop, the other hens and rooster ran out, but Gracie stayed in her nest box, silent and dull. I lifted her up and carried her out to the vegetable garden to be with the others. She kept apart from them, and after a few hours walked back to the coop and sat on an empty nest.

The can was a soup can, and nine kids were hunkered down around it: Donny Jamieson, Marcy and Robyn Strauss, my best friend Nancy Schmidt, me and my brother Alec, Ellen Pavanel, Kip and Susan Beckman. After the fathers came home from work, Westmount Road was deserted. Kip ran down the street in front of our homes, shouting with his whole being, then took aim and kicked that can. It went flying, maybe onto the sidewalk, chalked with hopscotch squares, maybe into the driveway where the boys let off firecrackers, maybe into that bramble patch on the corner where we all buried our dead pets with popsicle stick crosses. I didn't see where it went because, like all of them, I was racing to my hiding place. Behind the Strausses' garage, beside the Schmidts' hedge, crouched under the Beckmans' porch, heart pounding, hearing the sounds of the seeker, looking, calling, close to your hiding place, then, a surprising disappointment as the voice receded and diminished, now looking elsewhere, giving up on you. The others have been found. The mothers are calling from their front steps: "All in! Come on in! Time's up. Time to come on in."

That's an interesting moment. The hedge is wet and sweet smelling. You feel the contours of the warm human-hiding

earth beneath you, the cold, starry sky indifferent above you,
half-wishing you could live out here, undiscovered, forever, and
half-wishing a friendly and familiar face would suddenly poke
its way into your too-perfect hiding place and shout: "Got you!"

Why did I say Gracie was having a last kick at the can? She wanted more than life had allotted her. She wanted more eggs, she wanted more chicks, she wanted more time. When I woke in the night, sweating, throwing off the covers, twisting uncomfortably in my own skin, was I grieving the loss of my children, or was I also grieving the loss of myself as a child? Was I wishing I could turn the clock right back to the beginning? Sun still high above the horizon, can still in the middle of the road...

When I finally got her off the nest and back into the garden, she looked sickly in the cool autumn sunlight, her pink legs and pink comb unnaturally pale. The other hens scratched and pecked all day; she slept next to the cold frames. I could rouse her a little bit with chunks of corn on the cob, but the way she alternated between skittishness, when she was around the other chickens, and lethargy, when she was alone, scared me. I blamed myself. I let her sit on those eggs for what I now realized were selfish reasons, and I let her get run down when she should have been building up stores for winter. When she began her moult, I realized she wasn't strong enough for the change in season, colder days, freezing nights, and I became sure I would lose her.

But I didn't. She had a thorough moult, losing every one of her tail feathers until she looked like half a hen, and then began to rally. There were a few days she seemed exceptionally hungry, racing towards me if I came out with a few slices of bread, hanging out at the compost heap after the rest of the flock had gone back to the barn in the evening. She didn't advertise her finds: it's chicken etiquette to cluck if you've come on something worthwhile, but I watched her when she found the old honeydew melon in the compost, still full of sweet melon seeds, and she put it away without making a sound. The tail feathers grew back, blacker than they were before, and she even enjoyed a few days as "trophy wife," my nickname for the hen that gets the rooster's devotion for several days at a time, first pickings in the morning, close side-by-side roosting at night.

Well, that's Gracie's story; I started this bit of writing because I knew it was connected to mine. I let her sit on those dud eggs, late into the season, beyond what was good for her; fought a mink; brought her treats; worried about her; treasured her, because, sitting so persistently and instinctively on that nest, she just seemed the embodiment of maternal. I loved it, and I loved having a little share in it. Because I was out of eggs. That was the basic animal truth, and all the flashes, sweats, insomnia and crying jags were bringing it home. What kind of animal was I now?

The mothers have called us in. Some are angry and insistent. Some are laughing and indulgent. We won't give up the game just yet. Nancy takes a run at the can and sends it flying with a loud metallic clatter down the road, skips it sideways into the church parking lot. Alec has to run after it, get it—he's fast and it's still rattling—run it back to the middle of the road. Then he has to start searching for the hidden. If he searches away too far from the can, one of the hidden might spring from his or her hiding place and kick that can again. Then he's got to chase it down and put it back before he can restart his hunt. He's my brother, but it's a good game, and I'm the one leaping out of an excellent hiding place to kick that can to high heaven. Defy the mothers calling us in. Because this game's not over yet.

It helps me to remember that defiant young girl, racing away down Westmount Road. It was an awkward and painful transition when my body began using estrogen, so it's an awkward and painful transition to offload it, but I can do it, finding what felt good when I was a kid, where my deep energy came from, what was real, what mattered, what I cared about. And it helps me to think of Gracie, alias Vita, which means "life," so I must have been perceptive after all. I see her on top of the world, eating melon seeds, with a girly pink comb and a huge fan of striking black tail feathers, all her eggs, all her sacrifices, all her responsibilities gone, just being herself again.

....

SHEILA DEANE *grew up in Waterloo, Ontario, and continued her education at the University of Western Ontario, where she taught women's studies and English literature for many years. Her son and daughter are grown; she and her husband, Patrick, live west of Hamilton, where she enjoys weaving, gardening and writing.*

Have Genes Will Travel

CAROL BRUNEAU

Aided and abetted by my writing life, I've made a career of avoiding two things: mathematics and pantyhose. Pantyhose is too much like having your butt in a sling and math like having your brain in one. I was an advocate of denim through the rearing of three boys and the birthing of an indeterminate number of books, so until I turned fifty-one, the only kind of "genes" that mattered fell under the category of Gap, Lee or Paris Blues. Simply put, writing and rearing meant staying home, staying put. A simmering time during which I, ever a comfort hound, was quietly cooking for some metaphorical party that lay ahead, whatever the treats or feats it might involve and however long it lasted.

But this is not a piece about food. Too much food makes you fat, slows you down. When life after fifty, as we know, is about speeding up.

My mother, who loved math, detested cooking and never felt svelte enough to wear pants in public, considered pantyhose man's greatest invention—an invention her sister, my dear Aunt Bess, has never caught on to. Nor did Bess, who hates math, discover pants until deep into retirement. My mother died years ago, at age fifty-nine. At 103 Bess is still alive and kicking, most certainly one of the last of her garters-stockings-and-corset generation. (And I do not mean Madonna's accoutrements.)

I can say with utter confidence, though, that unlike Madonna and me, neither my mother nor Bess ever wore jeans. Besides their common gene pool, this may be the only way in which they were similar. My mother, a nurse, never left the Maritimes. Bess, a teacher, travelled the world. A jeans-uniformed Maritimer newly addicted to travel, perhaps I'm somewhere in between?

A go-getter from the start, Bess left their coal-mining hometown in Cape Breton at seventeen for art school in Halifax. She instructed people blinded in the Halifax Explosion in the art of basket-weaving. Shipping out on a coal boat, she designed neon signs in Quebec and tombstones in Toronto. The Great Depression pressed her into full-time teaching, starting with one-room schoolhouses, advancing to a girls' reformatory. Enlisting with the Women's Army Corps, she served in London all through the Blitz and was about to travel to the Orient when the bomb fell on Hiroshima. Returning home, she hitchhiked across Canada, then eventually settled into a teaching job in Halifax.

But this was just her simmering time, this woman born two days shy of half a century before me. The second oldest in a family of nine kids in which my mom was the second youngest. Bess marked turning fifty by being the first female to graduate from Saint Mary's University. A preamble to riding a camel to the pyramids of Giza, sharing illegal champagne with a customs man in Saint Pierre and Miquelon, petting lizards in the Galapagos and taking a cab to Silkeborg to see Denmark's Tollund bog man.

Teaching enabled these journeys but took away from her time for painting. Her living room was her studio, scented with turpentine, linseed oil and Yardley's lavender, canvases everywhere. A painter in oils, a reader of poetry, a piano player, she refused to let necessity get in the way of fun. She is and was a child at heart who taught art to Haligonian kids rich and poor in an era when school boards balked at buying manila. The inspiration and love of my ceramist sister's life, and of mine, she is and was the aunt who denied us colouring books but furnished all the paper, paint, books and music lessons our hearts desired *and* who nursed our mother through her long, agonizing illness.

A lady who at eighty-seven—properly attired, naturally, in a pretty print dress and stockings—climbed England's mystical Glastonbury Tor with us. She did it without blinking, ascending and descending the steep, corkscrew-terraced hill reputed to be the gravesite of Arthur and Guinevere. The legendary Avalon, entrance to the Land of the Fairies. A woman who by then had outlived her mother by three years.

Her life so packed with friendships and adventures a Kindle couldn't begin to hold it all.

The doctors ask, "What's your secret?" "Being single," says Bess, having never married, losing her one love to TB. One and one = one. Sharp as a whip, she's older than most of the buildings in town and much too beautiful to care. And although she is almost blind now, she still lives alone, quite independently, in her tidy white bungalow overlooking the harbour near her birthplace. Her days enlivened now by talking books and memories and a quiet faith—a joyful gratitude—though it is lonely, outliving all your contemporaries.

Urging me to see Italy, she dreams of visiting Iceland.

"Too bad Bess never married," people used to say to Mom, which would make her roll her eyes still, if she could.

For my mother never grew old. A feminist before it was cool to be one, she pitched her girdles and garters—jubilantly—when I was in grade seven. And died at the age I'm fast approaching, which is long past Go and beyond *Free Park-ing* but still pretty shy (I hope) of *Go to Jail*. She was spared, by an illness that mimicked Lou Gehrig's, of the sags and bags afflicted by aging. Sparing middle-age me the care of a sickly and/or senile senior—for which I'm sadly grateful, having cared for my elderly dad while raising teenagers. That is, if life's reversals and repetitions, its sums and subtractions, equal "fairness"; if dying can be considered a happy trade-off; and if fifty *is* the new forty, or thirty, or twenty—which Mom's dying and Bess's longevity have proved to me it has to be: life is far too short to waste fussing over wattles or fear or numbers.

Go for it, was the prompt that losing my mother issued. The hard nudge to follow the ways of Bess—well, except for her singleness. For I've been lucky in love, having had my husband longer than I had my mother; I've lived longer without than with her.

But maybe she speaks loudest in death? The silence of the urn far louder than the Betty Friedan paperbacks she'd leave lying around when I was a kid. Louder than the Nice 'n Easy boxes she stockpiled. The fifties' mom in our safe sixties' neighbourhood who didn't own a diamond; the one who taught the others to drive. A maternity nurse who called the Pill a male convenience (*à la* Germaine Greer); and no, Mom wasn't Catholic; she refused to convert, though doing so would have pleased my dad. A bright, funny, practical and calm woman with a melancholy edge who hungered for the world and envied Bess and her travels, longed to follow suit but never had the chance.

I will never forget her planning the trip of a lifetime with the nurses' union to the Soviet one, as it was back then, and getting sick. Her first doctor dismissed it as menopause, and it was downhill after that: ten years of tests, increasing paralysis and eventually the inability to feed or bathe herself or speak.

Her passport photo like a convict's from the Gulag: one who would not escape.

Yet in my mind, my mother is eternally forty, young for her age. Permed and lively, solid hipped, quick to laugh—that laugh charged with a Cape Bretoner's black humour, a nurse's humour—the woman who, without knowing, taught me from babyhood how especially sweet an orange tastes at the beach and how tangy cottage cheese with a splash of vinegar tastes at the kitchen table. Orange-peel/cottage-cheese thighs a total non-issue against the sparkle of sun, sea and sand.

Later, if she hated aging, if she suffered from hot flashes, I never knew it, too wrapped up in ponchos and blue jeans, Carole King, and boys to notice.

"I hope you'll never be silly like that," she once warned sternly, when, as a preadolescent, I was still too young to get what she meant. The pair of us on a walk in the woods, stumbling upon two teenagers, a girl and a boy, making out. I can still hear the timbre of Mom's voice, feel the danger in her smile. Because sex made girls do stupid things. It led, for instance, to the pregnant twelve-year-olds she saw at the hospital where she worked—my mathematically minded mother capped, dressed and hosed pristinely in white. One and one = three.

But even more complicated than its math, sex led to doormat-dom; this was the gist. Enslavement to makeup, bad backs due to high heels, pleasing, self-doubt—surrender. This from my mom, who, when I was really small, thought slacks looked trashy. My mom, who owned an eyelash curler and—at a time when white lipstick was the rage, never mind that it made its wearers look like corpses—wouldn't leave the house without her Cover Girl coral.

"Why?" I'd ask.

"Because it keeps me from looking tired," she'd say.

Like mother, like daughter?

Though very tired at the end, she feared and loathed and dreaded dying.

Afterwards, and for a long time—through most of my marriage, the births of my sons, their passage to (relative) adulthood—it was Mom's look that haunted me from the mirror. Before my hair got grey, before presbyopia made it impossible to apply eyeliner without the help of my glasses; when I hadn't a worry over wrinkles or wattles. It was her look that urged—enraged—me to write, my first book fuelled by the feeling of having been cheated. How could she leave me? Her loss seen through the eyes of a child until I had children of my own, and then only magnified by my own motherhood.

Her loss a stony, ongoing reminder of what happens when you wait, when you hesitate and for whatever reason don't seize the day. When you allow things to prevent you from seizing it.

Don't be silly.

"What's silly?" Bess would ask. My aunt who never lived with a man, never lived with anybody, and, though her vision is almost gone now, still looks for shapes—figures, not numbers—in the clouds.

"I don't know why I'm still here," she says, wondering why nothing (yet) has "carried" her "off," although she's had some close calls. Marvelling still, because she never thought she'd live longer than their mama.

Presbyopia, macular degeneration, cataracts—just a few of the slow, sad afflictions that detract from what the mirror reflects back at us all. The ticking time bomb of genes. More than that, an inner beauty.

To Bess, I'm virtually a tween. And maybe it's true; maybe we all are until we've outrun our mothers. The rest, then, borrowed time, gravy?

Superstition would give me six more years, and faith and imagination another fifty, depending on which side of the unilateral gene pool we dip into. Whose example I choose, a daily choice, blending gratitude with foreboding. Practicality with silliness. Realism with fancy. The glass neither half full at this side of fifty, nor half empty. Death made big by observing biology, or dwarfed by following the whims of imagination? The wisdom of weighing both.

The wisdom of Bess, of course, who—despite all my mother's coaxing, all Mom's vain attempts to convince her of the pluses of pantyhose, not to mention, later in her short life, pants—only started wearing slacks in her nineties. Then and only then she took to them as protection against the brambles in her backyard, the cliff-side tangle of wild rose and blueberry that to her is *Park Place* and *Boardwalk*.

I guess it is a privilege to travel so far and then come home. My own life mimicking this in a small way, somewhat circumscribed but I hope not abbreviated.

Seeing and not seeing.

Viewed without glasses, from the mirror my face glows these days, soft and wrinkle free: never mind that the details are fuzzy. An almost empty-nester, I'm a late bloomer: eager but not entitled. Knowing vaguely and with gratitude that these days, months, years (?!?)—the "downhill" stretch—are "payback" time, though it sounds obscenely presumptuous saying it. A burst of freedom after raising my boys and seeing my father through his dying days, all the duties and obligations that put things like trips on hold.

The resolution that this freedom brings: better late than never. The starting point, the mid-century mark. Whether the rest is an upward or downward slope, I take my cues from Bess, and though math has never been our friend, aided and abetted by its hard equations.

Live large, they dictate. Multiply joy: count every minute and make each one last. Which at present, right here, right now, boils down to this: one and one = two. Having simmered and stewed, the mix reduced to the two of us, my husband and me, firm in the fact that during our years of cooking, there was never the money or anyone to mind the kids to enable much flight.

Our idea of a trip, not long ago, back in those smaller,· slower days and lengthier years with their seemingly endless but endlessly vague spread of more ahead, was an overnight getaway here and there, to nice enough places that were horribly close by. Trips measured in kilometres and minutes.

Biding time. Gathering steam. Conserving gas.

But thanks to the hard math that accompanies aging, we've begun to catch up. To pull as many Besses as we can in whatever time we have left.

We started with Paris one April.

A repeat performance the following spring.

Our romance with France just the beginning.

This year it's Rome.

Though nothing can or will match the feeling, I'm sure, of seeing the Seine for the first time, of crossing the courtyard of the Louvre. Of eating smoked salmon under the flowering chestnuts in the garden at the Musée Rodin.

"Pinch me. Pinch me," I couldn't stop saying. "I must be dreaming."

Sampling lemon tarts in the Rue Montorgueil, *pain au chocolat* from Bon Marche, quiche from Rue Mouffetard… wine from Languedoc, camembert from Normandy…

All of it walked off quite easily at this age. The age of travelling without tampons. Comfy if not too chic in my sneakers and jeans.

But maybe this spring I'll wear snazzy tights, perhaps even heels. Making hay while the sun shines, strolling along the Appian Way. Which leaves me with one question: How *did*

Bess get around—admiring the wisteria at Versailles, hiking around the Isle of Skye, climbing Machu Picchu, trekking to Aztec temples, riding gondolas in Venice, crossing Piccadilly Circus—without popping or dropping a garter?

I'm sure she must've done both. And I know she got ladders—probably lots. She's just never worried too much about such details, even less about the shape of her legs underneath. "That's silly," she would say—will say—"as long as they work." Reminding me, "Whatever you do, dear, don't miss Florence."

CAROL BRUNEAU *is the Halifax-based author of two short story collections and three novels, including* Purple for Sky, *which won the 2001 Thomas Head Raddall Award for Atlantic Fiction and the Dartmouth Book Award, and* Glass Voices, *a* Globe and Mail *best book of 2007. She teaches writing at* NSCAD *and Dalhousie universities.*

I Feel Great about My Hands

SHARI GRAYDON

I n tribute to Nora Ephron, I called this collection *I Feel Great about My Hands*. If you're at all familiar with the *New York Times* Best Seller List, you probably already know: she feels bad about her neck.

I'd say suck it up, Nora, if I didn't find her so entertaining. But it's hard to feel a lot of sympathy for a happily married, successful Hollywood screenwriter and director who gets to work with Meryl Streep, Billy Crystal and Will Ferrell. (Okay, maybe not so much Will Ferrell; it's tough to imagine having a real conversation with Will Ferrell.)

Me, I feel bad about the fact that my increasing maturity has not translated into an ability to keep the hurricane zone I call my office better organized. I feel bad about people who regularly inject Botox into their brows, not realizing that after ten years of this vanity circus, the needle marks will start to show up on their foreheads like heroin tracks up a junkie's arms. (At least, that's what I imagine might happen, in my envious moments.)

I also feel bad about healthy young women who get breast implants as a graduation gift. I'm guessing they haven't considered the lifetime replacement costs, financial and otherwise. Nor do they realize that, although Grand Canyon cleavage is *in* now, in the 1920s, it was seriously *out*. (I credit French fashion designer Pierre Poiret, who authoritatively declared at the time, "The breast will no longer be worn." Judging from available photographs, I believe this was a tribute to his boyish-figured wife, so it's possible that what sounds, at first hearing, deeply misogynistic may actually have been mildly endearing. We'll just never know.)

But clearly, if shoulder pads, platform shoes and leg warmers can make fashion comebacks, why not small breasts? (And yes, I *am* hoping it happens in my lifetime.)

Ephron mourns having entered the turtleneck-wearing, Nehru-collar-sporting, scarf-demanding years. I just don't feel her pain. In my wardrobe, funky, elegant and colourful scarves rescue a multitude of fashion mistakes, offset my winter pallor and hide mid-life hickeys. (I definitely don't feel bad about those.) Besides, high-necked collars make me feel tall and regal, even though the only tall thing about me is my hands.

Did I mention I feel *great* about my hands?

They're as large as my husband's, and he's got five inches and sixty pounds on me. (In contrast—because I imagine some of you are now wondering this—my feet are considerably smaller.)

Big hands on a small woman may not sound like such a good thing. And when I first noticed their disproportionate dimensions as a late-blooming twelve-year-old—probably because not much else about me was growing as quickly as I'd hoped—I didn't exactly celebrate. In fact, arrested by one of the bust-exerciser ads then prevalent in the back of comic books, I considered that perhaps if I spent less time sketching and painting and more time doing push-ups, I could possibly redirect my body's growth hormones to a part of my physique more likely to enhance my social life.

But the prospect of cleavage and its ambiguous rewards weren't remotely enough to subvert my artistic calling. In my studio—a location the other members of my family insisted on referring to as my bedroom—I wove striking neckties from lime green and purple acrylic yarn, macraméd chic jute handbags and applied my emerging calligraphy talents to creating cringingly immodest signage for my door. (My siblings were quick to reinterpret "Shari the Great: Kneel" as "Shari, the Great Heel.")

But by fourteen, my beauty sacrifices had paid off, and my hands had also become adept at drawing impressively recognizable people from black and white photographs taken from LP covers and teen magazines. So true-to-life were these sketches that for years I was under the illusion that I might some day be able to retire on the proceeds of my celebrity portrait collection. I did realize at a certain point that Sylvester Stallone might prove to be less lucrative than originally thought, but Al Pacino and Paul McCartney continued to look like serious cash cows—should I ever need to sell them. (And then one day I was rudely awakened. Walking along a busy street in downtown Toronto, I discovered a community of immigrants who could not only whip up similar portraits in minutes but were prepared to let them go for the shockingly low price of fifty dollars.)

When I was a teenager, my dexterity was indispensable to my vision of adulthood (admittedly limited, it featured an imposing easel, an airy loft and an endless loop of The Moody Blues). And yet I cared about my hands the way a puppy cares about her paws: I completely took them for granted.

Fast forward a few years. It's 1979. I'm doing scene work in an acting class at university. Colleen, my best friend, has selected the play—an obscure one-act by Leonard Cohen called *The First Step*.

We've cast ourselves against type: although in reality, Colleen is the serial dater who loves men and leaves them with a kind of Casanova-like carelessness, I'm playing the pretty one with the boyfriend, and she's playing the pathetic loser.

I run around the stage in a slip, primping for my big date with the desirable man I'm convinced is about to propose. She follows me forlornly, demanding that I either confirm her ugliness or back up my contention that she has "good points."

"Name one point," she says.

Clearly grasping for a plausible compliment, my character lamely blurts out, "Your hands. You have nice hands."

We laugh at this in rehearsal, not only because it's a ridiculously insulting thing to offer under the circumstances, but because Colleen—she of the spectacular legs, beautiful pert breasts, luxuriously thick and glossy hair—did *not* have great hands. At least, not so as you'd notice. She bit her nails to the quick, worried the skin around them and then exiled her hands to pockets.

So we laugh even harder when her character says, "Yeah, sure: my hands. Men *come* when they shake hands with me."

And yet, even though hands are not the kind of attributes that teenage boys and middle-age bloggers typically rate on a scale of one to ten, they do offer the mature woman several advantages over other body parts when it comes to attracting attention.

You can't really reach out and touch someone with your breasts—well, not just anyone, and, frankly, not with mine. Plus, even if I hadn't watched half a dozen close friends undergo the trauma of losing one or both of theirs, the terrifying statistics make it abundantly clear: smart women don't get too invested in their breasts, because they may turn against you.

Hands, however, are not so vulnerable to disease. And they have the added advantage of being on display virtually all the time, regardless of how old you become. Unlike breasts, you can wave them in people's faces without being accused of indecorous behaviour. Unless you live in a nudist colony or make your living in the sex trade, beautiful breasts or spectacular buns must—on at least some occasions—be kept under wraps. Naked hands, however, are *de rigueur* at all hours of the day, every day of the week. (Okay, perhaps not so much if you spend your winters in seriously sub-zero temperatures. But even—or especially—here in the national capital, once you're inside, the gloves definitely come off.)

Recently, while speaking to a trio of federal bureaucrats in an attempt to wrangle vast sums of money to support a world-changing project, I noticed that one of the three was distracted by my gesturing hands. This was a bit disconcerting, because it appeared to be interfering with her ability to recognize the brilliance of my proposal. But trying to still my hands was risky; the older I get, the more seriously compromised my capacity to articulate becomes without their assistance.

In fact, when something inexplicably interrupts the synapses required to retrieve, let alone form, complex, technical terms such as "jar," "furnace" or the particularly challenging "paper tray," my hands frequently have to step in and take over. (Interestingly, my inability to call forth such words increases in direct proportion to my husband's impatience in filling the pause. And his guesses—"pancake?" "mail?" or "refrigerator?"—do nothing to hasten the process.)

Perhaps I should have stuck to shiatsu. For three years in my early twenties, I dedicated my hands to the mysterious art of acupressure massage, applying thumbs, knuckles and occasionally fists to points along the acupuncture meridians of strangers' aching backs. Words were mostly irrelevant. (I say "mostly" because one day, in the tatami room next to me, I heard the lovely and gentle Mitsue, fresh off the boat from Japan and still struggling with the unfamiliar "r" of her adopted country, asking a client, "Would you like more *plessure?*" Concerned about the precedent already set by our colleague Viv, who, ensconced in a much more private room upstairs, apparently offered "extras," the details of which we preferred not to know, I desperately wanted to shout, "No, Mitsue, no!")

Despite having cut short my careers in both visual art and shiatsu therapy, I remain financially dependent on my hands. Their capacity to assist my brain, on the far side of fifty, in translating random thoughts, arresting quotes and mind-numbing government briefing notes into books, articles and speeches keeps me fed. And the hours I spend hammering a computer keyboard makes my nails grow like teenagers—quickly and inconveniently. As a result, I keep them long and naked.

One December, temporarily separated from the love of my life and bluer than I'd ever been, I was standing at a courier counter in a last-ditch attempt to prove that I cared enough about my relatives to get their Christmas presents to them on time. The clerk assisting me stopped mid-sentence to gush over my hands, begging to know where I had my nails done. Although I'd been waiting decades for someone to appreciate my hands as much as I did, in my fantasy, the discovery would be made by a New York talent agent offering thousands of dollars in exchange for my indispensable aid in pursuit of increased hand lotion profits.

Incapacitated by the dashing of too many dreams, and apparently incapable of taking a compliment, I looked at the courier clerk stupidly and said, "Are you asking me who I pay to file my nails? Why would I *do* that?" But it was a measure of my desperation that I then re-lived the attention for weeks afterwards, reassuring myself that all was not lost. I may be forty-one and single, I thought at the time, but I still have my hands.

More recently, in a revelation that made my feminist heart pause, I learned that long nails are essentially the less debilitating European equivalent of Chinese foot binding. Even though mine are a *result* of my work, their impracticality apparently telegraphs a life of leisure. (As it happens, my writing wardrobe of yoga pants and pilling cardigan sweaters already does that.) But I'm unwilling to trim my nails; in my vanity, I imagine they do for my hands what stilettos do for other women's legs, causing them to appear slimmer and more graceful than they actually are.

Notwithstanding my own inability to walk a block in high heels, I also feel great about my feet.

You might not, if they were yours. I have—as my mother informed me at an impressionable age—my grandmother's bunions. This unasked-for paternal inheritance prevents me from performing a number of yoga poses, dancing *Swan Lake* with the National Ballet, and wearing what a former colleague used to call "fuck me" shoes.

But I'm good with that. I think stilettos are torture chambers invented by men who feel bad about women. I could speculate on why they want to punish us, but more to the point is how we'd like to pay them back.

In my fantasy, Manolo Blahnik and Jimmy Choo—over fifty and having worn out the cushioning flesh on the soles of their own feet—are both crammed into a pair of their implausible creations for an entire evening. I imagine them discovering their car battery dead and their wallets inexplicably empty of serious cash or credit cards. As a result, Manny and Jimmy have to run three blocks—along cobblestoned streets— to catch a bus. Every seat is taken, requiring them to stand for the thirty-seven-minute journey. Disoriented from the unaccustomed pain in their contorted metatarsals, they inadvertently disembark five stops too early and are forced to negotiate an additional nine ice-encrusted blocks. Barely surviving these with ankles, pelvic bones and dignity intact, their next challenge is to get from one end of the Metro Toronto Convention Centre to the other, carrying heavy winter coats and a sack of hammers each. (Never mind why; it's my fantasy.)

When the hapless shoe designers finally arrive at the stand-up cocktail reception, they're expected to ignore their bleeding toes and balance each of their aching pins on less than half a millimetre of support while juggling an overflowing martini glass, a small plate of precariously stacked hors d'oeuvres, and an evening clutch which—*zut alors!*—does not contain a single Band-Aid or pain reliever of any kind.

When they emerge from the experience crippled and crying for Epsom salts or cozy slippers, I don't feel bad about that, either. Nor do I offer to massage their feet, although clearly I could. Twenty-five years past the tatami room, my hands retain the capacity to knead and pummel their way into the good graces of hospitalized relatives, cottage-owning friends and the blissed-out man who rarely complains about paying the lion's share of our mortgage. This portable gift allows me to arrive anywhere without chocolates or wine and never feel empty handed. Whether I'm visiting my aging parents or former in-laws, for a weekend or merely lunch, they're delighted to forgo flowers for a temporary distraction from advancing aches.

And my intimate experience of older bodies reinforces other cautionary, motivating tales. Years ago, confronted by a tattered snapshot of my just-passed grandmother at a youthful sixteen—my own age at the time—I discovered that my incipient bunions were not the only things we shared. The woman I knew as overweight, arthritic and complaining, about whom I'd only recently penned a poem I cavalierly entitled "Born Old," was, as a teenager, shockingly familiar: the narrow face, large sad eyes and too-long nose—I was her twin in modern dress. My resulting vow to not go gentle into *her* good night was firm, if unconscious.

These days, dashing home from yoga to cook my vegetarian supper, I occasionally catch a glimpse of our fifty-something face reflected in a store window. And yes, it does momentarily freak me right out.

The rest of the time, now sporting her bequeathed diamond ring every day, instead of only on special occasions, I am grateful for the places my bony feet can still take me.

And I feel really great about my hands.

....

SHARI GRAYDON *is the award-winning author of two best-selling media literacy books for youth (*Made You Look, *on advertising, and* In Your Face, *on beauty culture). Currently leading* Informed Opinions, *a project to support expert women in bridging the gender gap in the public discourses, she's plotting a new collection, tentatively called* And Did I Mention My Legs?

Acknowledgements

A collection of writing is demonstrably the labour of many people, and I feel enormously privileged to have had the opportunity to collaborate with so many wonderful women whose thoughtful, funny, provocative and inspiring work appears here. I also appreciate the generosity of spirit shown by a number of others who drafted something that was fine and honest but didn't quite fit for one reason or another.

Janice Kennedy, whose deft and pointed columns on an impressive array of female-friendly topics have inspired me to write many positive letters to the editor over the years, was the first woman I spoke to about this book. Her immediate enthusiasm emboldened me to proceed.

The sympathetic professionals at Douglas & McIntyre, in addition to making it possible to share this book with the world in a beautiful package, allowed me necessary flexibility during a very difficult time.

My dear friend Renate Mohr brought an extra set of discerning eyes to the manuscript and its parts on a number of occasions when I needed fresh perspective; I am fortunate to benefit from her wise and reliable counsel.

My mother, Norma Graydon, in addition to explicitly encouraging me to look forward to my forties, modelled throughout her life the rejuvenating power of intense curiosity and a meaningful career.